The 100 Greatest Christmas Movies

Scott Speed

CONTENTS

INTRODUCTION

The book that follows contains one hundred Christmas themed movies and television specials that you should certainly consider watching during the festive season. The qualification for entry here is that each film should at least contain a Christmas scene or be set at Christmas. There are many perennial Christmas viewing staples like The Wizard of Oz and Willy Wonka and the Chocolate Factory but films like this don't qualify for our book because they aren't set at Christmas. Films like On Her Majesty's Secret Service and Night of the Hunter DO qualify though because they have references to Christmas. That's how our list works.

You'll find a very eclectic mix in the book that follows. Beloved television cartoons, comedy specials, obscure horror films, art house movies, action classics, stop-motion animation, anthology segments, and even a few bizarre or cheesy guilty pleasures. The list that follows is truly a case of the sublime and the ridiculous at times. The connective tissue though is always Christmas. So, put another log on the fire, get yourself a mince pie, and prepare to dive into the 100 Greatest Christmas Movies!

THE 100 GREATEST CHRISTMAS MOVIES

ALICE (1990)

Alice is a 1990 film directed by Woody Allen. Christmas trappings here? Well, you get a swanky Christmas party scene and eggnog. Alice revolves around Alice Tait (Mia Farrow), a bored Upper East Side New York housewife married to wealthy but shallow and inattentive stockbroker Doug (William Hurt). Alice spends her days shopping, undergoing pedicures, gossiping over lunch with her sterile rich friends and consulting with interior decorators. She dreams of doing something artistic or creative such as writing but soon decides this is a fantasy.

After suffering from some back pain, Alice, on the advice of her New Age yuppie friends, visits acupuncturist Dr Yang (Keye Luke) in Chinatown. Dr Yang has a mysterious cellar - rather similar to the one in Joe Dante's cult 1984 film Gremlins - and places her in a trance before prescribing four different types of herb. Each herb will have a different effect on Alice leading to various fantasy shenanigans and a revaluation of her life and values.

Inspired by Fellini's 1965 fantasy Juliet Of The Spirits, Alice, a 1990 film released by Orion Pictures, is a middle-ranking Woody Allen film that gave a pointer to the direction he would take in the nineties - more throwaway, lightweight efforts like Mighty Aphrodite or Everyone Says I Love You. These films are well made but forgettable relative to their author's long body of work. Alice is a pleasant enough experience while you are actually watching it.

In terms of tone, Alice is quite reminiscent to Allen's equally whimsical contribution to New York Stories - although that short film did reward the viewer with far more laughs and funnier comic situations. Overall it would be fair to say Alice does not quite hit the heights of earlier Woody Allen fantasy themed films like The Purple Rose Of Cairo.

It's fun of course to see the various magic herbs take effect on Alice and her life during the course of the film. One potion makes her completely uninhibited and flirt with Joe (Joe Mantegna), a saxophone player who has a child at the same school as Alice's children. Though a social rung down from Alice's husband Doug, Mantegna's character is more interested in performing jazz and having a fun, relaxed life than chasing money. We gather that Doug is incredibly rich through his Wall Street position but because the job and the pursuit of money is his life Allen makes us see how pointless and empty this can be. Joe will never be as rich as Doug but we'd rather be Joe if given the choice - especially Especially when Doug says things like "You have a nice personality and you know sweaters..." when asked to list the things he loves about Alice.

The film stresses the need to live your life by a set of decent values and not worry too much about chasing wealth for the sake of it. Alice is a fairly slight story although Allen does touch on some theological themes and guilt. It has been described as a lighter version of Another Woman, his 1988 Allen film where Gena Rowlands, just like Alice, reflected on her life and the decisions she'd made, as well as the process of change. The difference of course is that Another Woman was a bleak chamber piece whereas Alice is very throwaway Woody Allen. Both are interesting but different films that don't quite find the director at his most inspired.

Mia Farrow pulls off the slightly oblivious uppercrust housewife angle perfectly though and is a delight in some of the various strange situations Alice later finds herself in. Woody Allen said he got the inspiration for the character from the chic, incredibly wealthy housewives, invariably clothed in mink coats, who swanned around the exclusive area of

Manhattan that he resided in, struggling to fill their day with endless shopping, school runs, and lunches.

A potion in the film summons the ghost of Alice's first love, dead former boyfriend Eddie (William Baldwin), who, Superman and Lois Lane style, takes her for a ride over New York. It's somewhat novel to watch a Woody Allen film that required special-effects although, like A Midsummer Night's Sex Comedy, all done in a relatively restrained and modest manner. Beyond the excellent Mia Farrow, William Hurt is suitably convincing as the aloof Doug although he doesn't have what one could describe as a major role in the film.

The previously mentioned Alec Baldwin has that cameo as Alice's dead boyfriend brought back to life as a ghost in a Christmas Carol type sequence and Cybill Shephard has a scene-stealing part as a sniffy television producer. Bernadette Peters is also very good as a Muse who appears to Alice and tries to persuade her to be more artistic. Peters and Farrow have some decent bantering together and Allen gives them some amusing jokes and lines. Joe Mantegna is reliably solid in the film in his everyman but slightly suave style and Judy Davis, Bythe Danner, supermodel Elle Macpherson and Julie Kavner also make appearances.

Alice is a whimsical piece of arty fluff that is enjoyable enough but hardly classic Woody Allen - despite the fantasy flourishes and more cinematic evidence of his great love for (and interest in) magic. At over 100 minutes it possibly stretches its premise a tad too far but it does have first rate performances and, as ever, a carefully selected soundtrack. Woody Allen plays I Remember You with strings when Mia Farrow and Alec Baldwin dance together and little moments like this make Alice a worthwhile if unsubstantial experience.

AND ALL THROUGH THE HOUSE (1989)

"Ho, Ho, Ho, Kiddies. Just your old pal, the Crypt Keeper having a little holiday fun. Why else would I be in this get up, unless there was a Claus in my contract? In fact, I've got some Christmas goose for you. Goose bumps that is. A little terror tale, chock-full of holiday fear. I mean cheer, of course. So, get a gander of a Yuletide yelp-yarn that goes a little something like this: Twas the night before Christmas, and All Through The House..."

And All Through the House is an episode of Tales from the Crypt. Tales from the Crypt was a cult horror anthology television series based on the infamous and influential (everyone from Stephen King to George Romero grew up loving them) 1950s EC horror and suspense comics published by William Gaines. The enjoyably lurid and colourful comics (which were rather gruesome and risque, although tongue-in-cheek and with their own twisted sense of morality) offered all manner of deaths, monsters, zombies, murders, ghosts, and general macabre mayhem stirred by greed, lust and envy until parents began to notice what their children were reading and the comics were banned, even becoming the subject of Congressional subcommittee hearings.

The television series became something of a phenomenon after its debut in 1989 and ran for seven seasons until 1996. Why did it work so well? The show had very solid foundations right from the start with Richard Donner, David Giler, Walter Hill, Joel Silver and Robert Zemeckis as executive producers and was consequently able to attract some notable directors and actors. It was also a HBO cable show and so didn't have to worry about censorship.

There is of course our recurring host for each episode too (he performs the Rod Serling framing function if you will) - the

"Crypt Keeper", a very cheeky (I always think there is a bit of John Lydon in the Crypt Keeper) animatronic puppet (designed by Kevin Yagher of the "Chucky" films) who looks like a zombie and makes all manner of deliberately terrible puns ("It was so hack-citing, I actually got scared for a moment - I thought my heart had started...") as he introduces the story we are about to see. The Crypt Keeper works because he's such a likeable character. I think great credit must go to the puppeteers and John Kassir (who supplied the voice) for giving him so much personality.

And All Through the House was written by Fred Dekker and directed by Robert Zemeckis. This story was previously adapted for the screen in the Amicus compendium film Tales from the Crypt - that very British interpretation of some of EC's horror stories. The segment that most people remember from that movie is the one where Joan Collins is menaced in her house on Christmas Eve by an escaped lunatic dressed as Santa Claus. Well, here is that story again, only this time with an American setting and Robert Zemeckis behind the camera rather than Freddie Francis.

It's Christmas Eve and housewife Elizabeth (Mary Ellen Trainor) puts her young daughter (played by Lindsey Whitney Barry) to bed and then whacks her unsuspecting husband Joseph (Marshall Bell) over the head with the fireplace poker. The murderous Elizabeth is after the life insurance but she has missed a local news bulletin about a dangerous escapee (played by Larry Drake) from the asylum who is at large and dressed as Father Christmas. When Elizabeth is attacked by the escapee outside she manages to get back inside and lock the door. Only then does she realise that she left the body of her murdered husband out in the snow. It means she can't call the police and must now deal with this deranged Father Christmas alone.

And All Through the House does unavoidably lose the element of surprise if you've seen the Amicus film but this is still well worth watching and is regarded by many to be one of the best

Tales from the Crypt episodes. The main difference with this one is that they open it up more with some of the action taking place in the yard outside. The Amicus adaptation was strictly Joan Collins in her house and had more claustrophobia.

While it looks like a slam dunk to cast Larry Drake as a murderous Father Christmas (and it is a slam dunk because Drake is great here) I do feel the Santa in the Amicus film was scarier because we hardly saw him save for a grubby bearded face at the window. Anyway, both versions are perfectly fine and this one is certainly fun too - especially if you are completely new to And All Through the House in any form.

AN AFFAIR TO REMEMBER (1957)

An Affair to Remember was directed by Leo McCarey and is a remake of McCarey's 1939 film Love affair. An Affair to Remember is an unashamedly romantic weepie in which Cary Grant and Deborah Kerr play a couple of people who fall in love after meeting on a cruise ship. Grant is a painter named Nickie Ferrante while Keer is piano teacher Terry McKay. The prospective romance between the two is complicated though by their private lives and careers but they agree to meet up atop the Empire State Building in six months time if they have sorted out their own affairs sufficiently to make a romance between them work. However, this rendezvous does not quite according to plan. Will everything turn out ok in the end though? Well, you can probably hazard a guess that love might just conquer all before the end credits roll.

An Affair to Remember is one of those cosy 1950s CinemaScope films which has wonderful locations and interiors and two great stars. Cary Grant could probably have played this sort of role in his sleep - it's almost as if he was genetically engineered in a lab somewhere purely to be a

Hollywood romantic leading man! Though some people tend to kock Grant's acting the great thing about this legendary star is that he always gave his characters a great sense of humour and was just naturally witty onscreen. Keer is a classic leading lady too and more than holds her own against Grant.

An Affair to Remember is sentimental and fluffy but it doesn't really matter because we just enjoy being in the company of these two actors. There's a bit of story with an element of tragedy thrown in but we are never in too much doubt that this romantic duo are going to find each other once more in the end. The film builds to a memorable last act set at Christmas Eve and so An Affair to Remember is not just a great romantic bauble of the era but also a Christmas film! There is also plenty of sass in the script to mitigate the schmaltz and Grant is at the height of his powers as the artist playboy Nickie. An Affair to Remember is a very classy and enjoyably picture and generally regarded to be one of the best romantic films ever to come out of Hollywood.

THE APARTMENT (1960)

The Apartment is Billy Wilder's peerless comedy drama about the put upon C.C. "Bud" Baxter (Jack Lemmon), an office worker at a New Yorker insurance company who allows his married bosses and seniors to use his apartment for romantic trysts with their secret girlfriends. Baxter hopes that this will help him climb up the corporate ladder - and it does in the end. However, this all comes at a price. None of this makes Baxter feel good about himself.

Matters become complicated too when Baxter discovers that Fran (Shirley MacLaine), the elevator operator at his office who has a crush on and would love to go on a date with, is secretly having an affair with his boss Mr Sheldrake (Fred MacMurray). Sheldrake is one of the men using Baxter's apartment for secret trysts. Will Baxter show some backbone and become a "mensch", as his cranky but kind neighbour Dr Dreyfuss (Jack Kruschen), demands, and, more to the point, will he ever win the heart of Fran?

The Apartment begins with Jack Lemmon in fine comic form as he deals with the complicated chaos of letting everyone at work use his apartment for their secret affairs. You expect this to be a comedy on the strength of this opening but the film becomes much more than. In fact, the dramatic elements take the film to some dark places - like when Fran overdoses in Baxter's apartment in dismay at the fact that Sheldrake is never going to leave his wife for her. It will be up to the memorable Dr Dreyfuss to save Fran.

There's a great cast here and Jack Lemmon is highly impressive in the way that he elicit laughs and can play farce but then also be completely convincing in the dramatic scenes. Shirley MacLaine is great too and this must surely rank as one of her best ever roles. The film depicts the corporate rat race of work as shallow and undignified. Baxter thinks that if he can get to the top (his cherished dream is to have a key to the executive washroom) then he'll have everything he ever wanted but it turns out that life isn't this simple.

The Apartment definitely qualifies as a Christmas film as there are scenes depicting Christmas Day in particular. We see Sheldrake at home with his family and his kids opening their presents. Fran is sad because she knows that Sheldrake would never spend Christmas Day with her. He's happy to keep her as a secret mistress but he'd never leave his family - unless they left him first. That's the sort of shallow man he is.

The Apartment is a brilliant film. It's hard to think of any Hollywood film that ever balanced comedy and drama so deftly. This is definitely a film that everyone should watch - especially at Christmas.

ARTHUR CHRISTMAS (2011)

Arthur Christmas is a 2011 animated film made by Sony
Pictures Animation and Aardman Animations. Aardman
Animations are of course most famous for the Wallace &
Gromit films. The premise of the film is that Santa Claus and
his family only manage deliver all the presents to children in
the world through high technology and a giant spaceship like
craft manned by hundreds of elves. It's a military type
operation on Christmas Eve to get all the gifts delivered and
the days when Santa did this with his trusty sleight and
reindeers are long gone.

The role of Santa Claus is passed down through the
generations of this family so that Father Christmas is
essentially immortal. One Christmas, there is a mishap in this
elaborate Christmas operation and one present remains on the
ship undelivered. The present was destined for a little girl and
young Arthur Christmas (voiced by James McAvoy) is
distraught by this oversight and decides that he must do
something about it. Grandsanta (voiced by Bill Nighy), who
was once Santa Claus but is now retired, decides to help
Arthur deliver the present and it will have to be done in the
traditional way - with reindeer and sleigh. The trouble is
though that Grandsanta is a bit out of touch with the modern
world and a fish out of water to say the least.

Arthur Christmas is a thoroughly pleasant and enjoyable
Christmas film with beautiful art and animations and a witty
script. The voice cast is great too. McAvoy and Nighy are
terrific and excellent support comes from Hugh Laurie,
Michael Palin, Jim Broadbent, Imelda Staunton, and many
others. You can be forgiven if you sometimes feel like you've
had to endure a few too many of these family animated films
but Arthur Christmas has enough invention and charm to
justify its own existence and stand out somewhat from the
pack. The music is really good too. If you like Christmas and
animated films then you can't go too far wrong with this film.

One could even argue that Arthur Christmas actually deserves to be more famous than it actually is.

BABES IN TOYLAND (1934)

Based on Based on Victor Herbert's popular 1903 operetta Babes in Toyland and directed by Gus Meins and Charley Rogers, this 1934 feature length picture has become a firm Christmas favourite with audiences and contains plenty to reward Laurel & Hardy fans. Stannie Dum and Ollie Dee reside in Toyland where they live in a giant shoe (!) with assorted characters from nursery rhymes. They work for the Toymaker (William Burress) but complications arise when they make the toy soldiers six feet tall instead of the usual fraction of that size. Stay tuned for the end though on this front! Our heroes determine to help Mother and Bo Peep (played by Florence Roberts and Charlotte Henry respectively) when the terrible landlord Silas Barnaby (Henry Brandon) threatens to make them homeless.

Laurel & Hardy's greatest strength was that they were were very human and the audience could recognise these failings in themselves. People like the Marx Brothers and WC Fields were more complex as acts than Laurel & Hardy and therefore inspired more extremes in terms of reactions. Laurel & Hardy's humour is accessible and timeless. Their motifs were comic violence and Hardy's look of quiet exasperation directly into the camera whenever some calamity had befallen him.

Babes in Toyland is arguably the best of Laurel & Hardy's opera outings thanks to some wonderful production design and costumes and plenty of amusing capers for the duo to engage in. The world realised in the film anticipates The Wizard of Oz in a sense and - like that classic - even has some scares in the form of the genuinely creepy Bogeymen. All in all, Babes in Toyland is one of the most memorable of Laurel & Hardy's longer features.

Another Laurel & Hardy Christmas themed film worth a look is Big Business. This is a James Horne short from 1929 and easily one of the best and most famous of their silent pictures. The pair play Christmas tree salesmen determined to impress the cantankerous James Finlayson. This leads to all out tit for tat war in the vein of their later battles with Charlie Hall. Big Business is hugely inventive and provides much comic spectacle.

BATMAN RETURNS (1992)

Yes, this is the Batman film with a Christmas backdrop! Despite the huge success of Batman (first picture to hit $100 million in only ten days), Tim Burton was not terribly excited about doing another one and later admitted he personally felt the 1989 film wasn't that great. Warner Bros wanted an immediate sequel and paid a fortune to maintain the Gotham sets at Pinewood but Burton went off to make Edward Scissorhands instead. He was enticed back for 1992's Batman Returns by the promise of more creative input and so this one has much more of a Tim Burton sensibility than the first one. The characters are more grotesque, Elfman's score is much more, well, Danny Elfman, it snows, there are circus performers and clowns as henchmen, an army of penguins, etc. I could go on but you get the general idea. It's just weirder than the first one.

The script Burton liked the most and chose to do was written by Daniel (Heathers) Waters and featured the Penguin and Catwoman. You suspect that part of the reason Burton liked the script was because it had absolutely no story whatsoever! It begins with a deformed boy (flippers for hands etc) terrifying his wealthy parents so much they throw him in Gotham's river where he ends up in the sewers and is raised by penguins.

Many years later he resurfaces as Oswald Cobblepot (Danny DeVito) and blackmails dodgy billionaire Max Shreck

(Christopher Walken) into helping him look for his parents. Or something. Shreck has plans of own that include stealing Gotham's electricity with a new power plant and decides that Cobblepot as Mayor would speed this process up. The present Mayor (Michael Murphy) therefore finds himself constantly assailed by Cobblepot (aka the Penguin) and his army of grotesque circus acrobat henchman.

Meanwhile, Shreck pushes his dowdy and meek secretary Selina Kyle (Michelle Pfeiffer) out of his skyscraper when she uncovers dodgy corporate secrets about him. She survives the fall but it causes a psychotic break in her personality. Inspired by her love of cats, she adopts a vinyl PVC costume and slinks about at night with a whip calling herself Catwoman. Catwoman teams up with the Penguin against Batman but matters are further complicated by her romancing Bruce Wayne (Michael Keaton again) as Selina Kyle - neither aware of the true identity of the other...

Batman Returns is slicker than the first film and more colourful to look at. It also moves at a faster clip and has more characters. While the film is often more entertaining than the first one though it does have some big problems. Burton decided not to return to the huge outdoor Gotham sets at Pinewood and shot Batman Returns in a Hollywood studio. The film seems very studio bound and constrictive at times. Presumably this was deliberate but about a third of the film seems to take place in a set which depicts Gotham square in the centre of the city. You start to yearn for the film to be opened up somewhat in the end. The film feels very artificial and is essentially hollow beneath the visual flourishes and Teutonic machine age design (which is pretty spiffy at times).

Sadly, Danny DeVito's Penguin does not really work here. The comic book character was a refined upper class criminal mastermind with a fondness for umbrellas and birds (the feathered kind). Burton was inspired by The Cabinet of Dr Caligari and reimagines the Penguin as a freak show performer. Richard III raised in a sewer. DeVito does his best under all the zombie cartoon make-up and prosthetics but he just isn't as funny or scary as Nicholson's Joker. His best scene I think is one where he gains control of Batmobile while Batman is driving and appears on a monitor to goad the Caped Crusader, complete with huge steering wheel as if he is playing a computer game. The film could have done with more of this.

It's part of the most exciting sequence in the film where Batman does battle with dozens of the Penguin's circus goons with his Batmobile, fighting skills and an assortment of gadgets. Some nice touches here but Burton, generally, is not an action director and so these films never quite hit the mark in this area. Incidentally, Batman seems to actually kill a lot of these henchmen in Batman Returns!

The Penguin's big criminal scheme here is a Damien Thorn style plot to kill all of Gotham's first born children. Charming! "My dear penguins, we stand on a great threshold! It's okay to be scared; many of you won't be coming back. Thanks to Batman, the time has come to punish all God's children! 1st, 2nd, 3rd and 4th-born! Why be biased? Male and female! Hell, the sexes are equal with their erogenous zones blown sky high! Forward march! The liberation of Gotham has begun!"

Pfeiffer looks great as Catwoman of course and purrs some of the best lines in the film ("Saved by kitty litter!") but her character is vague with a baffling story arc. One minute she is fighting Batman and the next minute she is trying to kiss him. It never really makes any sense. She's mad I suppose. That's the point. Walken's Max Shreck (horror buffs will get the joke) doesn't really work. He has a ridiculous fright wig and looks like he's stepped out of another century.

With so many supporting characters and three villains, Michael Keaton as Batman can't help but appear rather lost and overshadowed in his own film but he's very good again and suitably brooding as Bruce Wayne. He has some nice little moments with Michael Gough's Alfred again too. Believe it or not, the original plan was to have Robin in this film too. Robin was to be reimagined a streetwise black mechanic. Marlon Wayans was cast and got as far as a costume test before they decided that adding Robin was too much to a film that already had too many actors and characters for its own good.

The romance between Bruce Wayne and Selina Kyle is generally well played although it continues the incredibly downbeat and nihilistic aura that permeates the film. Both are so damaged they can't really ever be themselves. They have to have alter egos. When we see them at a costumed ball as the only ones ones not covering their face the message is clear. They wear a mask all the time even when they aren't Batman or Catwoman. Batman Returns, like the first film, ends up as less than the sum of its parts. There is some amazing stuff in Batman Returns if you can live with the absence of a plot, some clunky dialogue and far too many supporting characters. Just don't expect this film to cheer you up though. It's very melancholic!

THE BEAR (1998)

The Bear is a seasonal television animated film based on the dreamily illustrated 1994 children's book by Raymond Briggs. The Bear is much in the vein of The Snowman (although didn't quite enjoy the same success) and could be described as a sort of cross between that earlier Briggs book and The Tiger Who Came to Tea. As the title suggests, the story is about a bear, in this case a big fluffy polar bear who climbs through the bedroom window of a little girl called Tilly one night. Far from being afraid, Tilly invites the bear to stay and they become firm friends. Looking after a bear though, while a lot of fun, is also difficult work. How long will the bear stay before it thinks about going home?

The Bear is a decent enough attempt to recapture the spirit of The Snowman and although a lovely film it doesn't quite have the magic of that earlier favourite. There are a few key differences between the book and the film. The film removes the dialogue and relies on music and it also inserted a new section where the Great Bear constellation in the night sky guides the polar bear in a poignant but very flowery sequence.

The Bear leaves a few deposits around the house here, Briggs eager to remind us of a few of the potential pitfalls to living with a polar bear, and it wouldn't quite be Raymond Briggs without a few flourishes of a scatological or bittersweet nature that his publishers could probably have happily lived without. I gather that the bear doing his business around the house was originally left out of the Channel 4 film version but then put in at Briggs' insistence!

Like The Snowman, The Bear has a dreamlike quality with the misty, ephemeral animation and the strange and magical friendship at the heart of the story, a friendship of course that could never happen like this in the real world. One could say that the bear doesn't have as much personality as the snowman and is rather blank but I think most children will just be interested by the idea of a giant fluffy bear living in the house and not be too concerned about this.

The Bear is a nice, sweet film with some lovely sequences. Like The Snowman, The Bear is rather bittersweet with a very Raymond Briggs ending and there's a little moral message in there about animals. The relationship between the bear and Tilly is always touching and supplies the basis for various capers between the pair like the little boy and the snowman. The film has a nice wintry atmosphere too and the interiors of Tilly's house are drawn to look wonderfully cosy and warm. The Bear is definitely worth watching.

BETTER WATCH OUT (2016)

Better Watch Out (aka Safe Neighborhood) is a horror thriller directed by Chris Peckover. It is Christmas in a wealthy suburb

and teenager Ashley (Olivia DeJonge) has to babysit
twelve year-old Luke Learner (Levi Miller). However, this
turns out to be a nightmarish night for Ashley indeed because
Luke is no ordinary boy. To say too much more would be to
give the story away.

Better Watch Out features Christmas Carols and takes place
entirely in a house filled with Christmas decorations. It is
definitely then what you could call a Christmas thriller. The
film got pretty good reviews but tends to divide audiences.
Some people love this film and some hate it. One can
understand this polarisation because Better Watch Out is
definitely not going to be everyone's cup of tea and has a twist
that will probably alienate some viewers.

The film's first section sets the story up as a home invasion
thriller and as far as home invasion thrillers go it is gripping
and tense and all very entertaining. But then the movie
suddenly pulls the rug out from under the viewer and turns
into a completely different film. It seems that a lot of viewers
would have been happier if it had just stuck to being a home
invasion thriller. To say what the film turns into would be
giving too much away and although it's all well done the story
does rather strain credibility in the end and has some gaping
plot holes.

This is a rather nasty film at times - so it won't be for everyone.
You'll be rooting for one character in particular to get their
comeuppance and although there is some cosmic karma at the
end one can't wishing the final scene had been a bit more, well,
FINAL - as opposed to ambiguous. The cast is very good in this
film - especially Olivia DeJonge as the babysitter. Though set
in America the film was made in Australia with a mostly
Australian cast. Look out for Stranger Things star Dacre
Montgomery is a smallish part.

There are two American names in the cast though in the form
of Patrick Warburton and Virginia Madsen (of Candyman
fame) as the parents. Warburton is nicely droll in his scenes.

Better Watch Out is both compelling and infuriating in equal measure. It's a pretty solid Christmas thriller but it definitely won't be for everyone.

BLACK CHRISTMAS (1974)

Black Christmas is a horror film directed by Bob Clark. It was made on a low-budget in Canada and got very sniffy reviews when it first came out. These days though Black Christmas is considered to be a cult classic and a pivotal film in the horror genre. This was one of the first examples of the 'slasher' film and hugely influential. John Carpenter's Halloween was largely inspired by Black Christmas.

The film takes place in a college sorority house just before Christmas. The girls in the house are being plagued by strange phone calls by a 'heavy breather'. The mysterious caller eventually threatens to kill them and, this being a horror film, they should probably take his warnings seriously. This film has a fantastic Christmas atmosphere but uses the festive trappings to be sinister rather than magical.

The weird phone calls are alarmingly creepy and Black Christmas is a pretty decent thriller in that there are a few red herrings and some misdirection. This film is certainly creepy but it isn't caked in blood or that gruesome at all. It's more about suspense than nasty kills or blood and guts. There's a decent enough cast here despite the low-budget of the film. Margot Kidder, about four years before she was cast as Lois Lane in the Superman movie with Christopher Reeve, has plenty of sass and charisma as Barb and Olivia Hussey is the nominal lead as Jess.

There is also the ever dependable John Saxon as Lt. Fuller. Black Christmas is wonderfully effective in what it sets out to do and stacks up very well against the slew of stalker/slasher films which followed in its wake. It's rather perplexing to be honest that the film didn't get much acclaim when it first came out. The constrictive setting also works to the advantage of the film. if you are looking for something spooky to watch on Christmas Eve then Black Christmas is certainly recommended if you've never seen it before.

BLACKADDER'S CHRISTMAS CAROL (1988)

Blackadder's Christmas Carol is a one-off special 1988 festive edition of the famous Rowan Atkinson comedy show and was written by Richard Curtis and Ben Elton. In this special, Atkinson is Ebenezer Blackadder - a Victorian shopkeeper. Ebenezer is the nicest man in England but because of his kind nature is taken advantage of by all and sundry. Relatives, charity collectors, and the like chisel him out of his presents, tree, money, and even his Christmas dinner!

One night, Ebenezeer is visited by the Spirit of Christmas (Robbie Coltrane) and shown what his ancestors (from Blackdder II and Blackadder the Third) were like. Ebenezer notes that his sarcastic, scheming, and wicked ancestors actually seemed to be more successful than him! He starts to wonder if that old adage about nice people finishing last is really true. He is then shown visions of the future and decides to change his ways. Ebenezer no longer wants to be nice and kind. He wants to be like his wicked ancestors instead!

Blackadder's Christmas Carol is a fun seasonal bonus episodes for fans of this classic show and it's a nice twist to have Blackadder be all nice for a change - though this state of affairs obviously isn't going to last very long. Blackadder comes to conclude that nice people get nowhere in life but by the end of the story he might find that that isn't necessarily the case. There's a nice Victorian atmosphere here and it's fun too to see Atkinson play the Blackadders from previous series of the show. Happily, all the regulars from the show are here so you get Tony Robinson as Baldrick, Hugh Laurie, Stehpen Fry, Miranda Richardson, and Miriam Margolyes. Look out too for Doctor Who star Nicola Bryant.

Blackadder's Christmas Carol is perfect Christmas viewing and great fun.

THE BLUE CARBUNCLE (1968)

The Blue Carbuncle is an episode of the 1960s Sherlock Holmes television series featuring the great Peter Cushing. This was a continuation of a series that had started earlier in the sixties with Douglas Wilmer in the lead role. Wilmer's interpretation remains highly regarded and he had an uncanny physical resemblance to the literary character but he declined to return for the new series when he learned that the rehearsal time would be scaled back and the shooting schedule would most likely be brutal.

The BBC then offered the role to John Neville (who had played Holmes in the 1965 film A Study in Terror) but when he was unavailable due to existing theatrical commitments they turned to Cushing - who had of course already played Holmes before too in the wonderfully melodramatic and atmospheric 1959 Hammer version of The Hound of the Baskervilles.

The really sad thing about this series is that Peter Cushing shot sixteen 50 minute Holmes adventures but only six remain for us to enjoy today. It sounds completely insane now and artistic vandalism but this was the era when the BBC would often tape over their own shows to save money and much was lost forever. Cushing was rather old to be playing Holmes by now but he's still spry and (with sometimes darkened hair) his gaunt features are very Strand illustration and Holmesian.

He's more avuncular here than he was as Holmes in the

Hammer film but still laces the character with the appropriate arrogance and some semblance of depth. He's just a joy to watch at times dashing around looking for clues and juggling with props and I would certainly place him at the top table with Rathbone, Jeremy Brett and Robert Stephens.

The Blue Carbuncle was directed by Bill Brain and might be the most purely enjoyable of the sixties Cushing adventures. This is a festive story and as someone who is very familiar with the Jeremy Brett version it was fun for me to see a slightly different incarnation with Cushing and Stock. The story revolves around a £20,000 Blue Carbuncle jewel stolen from Lady Morcor (Madge Ryan). The prime suspect is John Horner (Neil Fitzpatrick) - one of the hotel workers where it was stolen - but perhaps all is not what it appears to be on the surface.

When a late night spot of fisticuffs is interrupted by a policeman (Frank Middlemass), he takes a goose and hat left at the scene to Sherlock Holmes. Holmes uses his extraordinary deductive skills to paint a profile of the man who owns the hat and gives the goose to Peterson. This is merely the start of this Christmas tinged goose themed mystery. Will Holmes solve the riddle of the stolen Blue Carbuncle?

This is not as Christmassy as I'd hoped it would be but it's still charming at its best and stacks up fairly well against the Granada version. The restrictive interiors become increasingly cosy as you settle into and get used to this series and that's certainly the case here. Cushing is fun of course in the famous scene where he deduces all manner of facts about a man just from his hat (!) and then invites Watson to do the same. Madge Ryan is a bit ripe as Lady Morcor but the supporting cast does some good work here and there are a couple of familiar faces.

The wonderful Michael Robbins (Reg Varney's sarcastic brother-in-law from On the Buses) as the trader Albert

Breckinridge and Dad's Army star James Beck (the spiv one with the mustache who sadly died very young in real life) as James Ryder, a key character in the unfolding events of the story. Both are excellent. I think the reason why The Blue Carbuncle works here is that the story is a more intimate, almost whimsical one, and this suits the nature of the production on this series.

The cosiness factor is amped up to a mug of hot chocolate and two crumpets by a crackling log fire and you don't really care about the fact that they clearly had precious little money to make this series. The Christmas overtones are of course delightful too and I wish they had expanded this somewhat into a full blown Victorian Christmas heavy caper. The Blue Carbuncle is still very pleasant and watchable though.

BRAZIL (1985)

You wouldn't really have Terry Gilliam's surreal dystopian nightmare film Brazil pegged as an obvious Christmas movie but it has plenty of Christmas imagery and uses the trappings of Christmas as a contrast to the grim world presented in the film. Gilliam uses Christmas in Brazil to remind us of the tension between fantasy and reality and this tension becomes a common theme throughout the film. The film has Jonathan Pryce as Sam Lowry, a lowly worker in a totalitarian state which owes a lot to George Orwell's 1984. Brazil is also what you might describe as Kafkaesque. The world depicted in the film is so bureaucratic that no one has the faintest idea what is going on!

The plot, such as it is, takes place just before Christmas and revolves around Sam trying to find a woman (Kim Greist) he has been having vivid dreams about. There isn't too much of a plot in the film though and it plays out in a series of often bizarre vignettes as Sam struggles to navigate this petty and miserable world. Brazil is definitely not going to be everyone's cup of tea but it is an amazing looking film and always quite compelling. What helps too is that it has a great cast with the likes of Robert De Niro and Michael Palin in support.

This film had a famously troubled release because the studio didn't really understand the film and wanted Gilliam to change the ending to make it less downbeat. Gilliam predictably refused so the studio did their own cut - much to Gilliam's understandable annoyance. In the end Gilliam was allowed to release his version after it was well received by critics. This is a pretty bizarre film but a memorable one too. This is definitely one of the stranger Christmas themed films you are ever likely to encounter.

CAMPFIRE TALES (1991)

A low budget anthology written and directed by William Cooke and Paul Talbot and not to be confused with the 1997 anthology of the same name. Despite the low-budget this is watchable nonsense with some enjoyable old fashioned gore effects. The wraparound has Gunnar Hansen joining some kids around a campfire to spin these spine chilling yarns...

The first story is another variation on 'The Hook' with a couple menaced by the usual horror film maniac. Despite the overly familiar nature of this segment it's not a bad opening story. They don't have much money at their disposal in terms of the look of this film but there's a certain bargain basement sense of fun that manages to filter through now and again and make you less grudging towards the compendium as an overall enterprise.

Story two involves two pot heads looking for marijuana and buying some from a weird dealer. The pot turns people into a gloopy mush. This segment doesn't make much sense and is rather on the skimpy side when it comes to story or explanations. I suppose the central premise is strange enough to be compelling though. I was intrigued enough to stay to the end even if nothing really blew my socks off ultimately.

The third story is an Amicus style tale of a man who murders his mother for her inheritance and faces the wrath of Satan Claus - a legendary character who dishes out justice to those who commit nefarious sins during the holiday season. It's predictable but fun. I'm not sure that Satan Claus is ever going to join the pantheon of horror icons but it's always quite entertaining to spin a horror story around Christmas as Christmas does have an enjoyably ghostly dead of winter type atmosphere when you come at the festivities from a slightly different (and skewed) perspective.

The last story involves a shipwrecked pirate who ignores warnings that treasure is guarded by zombies. You can probably guess how this one ends up. He's going to go after the treasure regardless and as this is an anthology horror film that's going to be a very big mistake. This story seems to be inspired by John Carpenter's The Fog and is a trifle on the long side. I think perhaps this one could have been tightened a little as we can all guess how it will end long before we reach the resolution. Like all the stories here though it passes the time. Campfire Tales is no lost classic but the makers of the film clearly have a lot of affection for the anthology genre. This is generally undemanding fun.

CAROL (2015)

Carol is a drama directed by Todd Haynes. The film is set in 1950s New York at Christmas and concerns young Therese Belivet (Rooney Mara), an aspiring photographer working in a department store. When an older woman named Carol Aird (Cate Blanchett) comes in the store to buy a gift for her daughter she ends up leaving a glove there. Therese arranges to have it sent to Therese. The two women meet up and have a romantic affair but matters are complicated by the fact that

Carol is married and being gay in the 1950s is a lot more difficult than it is today.

Carol was one of the best reviewed films of 2015 and many were bewildered that it was snubbed when it came to Oscar nominations. The film has great performances and a rich period atmosphere. It also has some fantastic Christmas scenes. There is just something amazingly Christmassy about period New York in films set during the festive period. Carol is a beautiful looking film with a great music score.

This probably won't be a film for everyone because of its low-key nature and sedate pacing but it's a very elegant and absorbing film which takes a sobering look at an era when society tended to be a lot more close minded and prejudiced about same sex relationships. The performances alone make Carol very worthy of your time and the beautiful photography makes Christmas almost like an extra character in the movie.

THE CHANGING OF THE GUARD (1963)

"Professor Ellis Fowler, a gentle, bookish guide to the young, who is about to discover that life still has certain surprises, and that the campus of the Rock Springs School for Boys lies on a direct path to another institution, commonly referred to as the Twilight Zone."

The Changing of the Guard is a Twilight Zone episode directed by Robert Ellis Miller and written Rod Serling. The Twilight Zone, possibly the greatest television series ever made, ran from 1959 to 1964 for 156 episodes and remains an enduringly iconic part of American popular culture. It was created by Rod Serling - who also wrote many episodes and always presented an introduction monologue to camera ("Submitted for your perusal...") before ending each fantastical tale with a closing piece of narration in his distinctive voice. The series was alternately spine chilling and poignant as each week a variety of unsuspecting characters took a wrong turn into the Twilight Zone, a place where anything could and often did happen.

The Changing of the Guard is one of the handful of episodes in the original Twilight Zone which was set at Christmas. In the story a veteran teacher named Professor Fowler (Donald Pleasance) is distraught and suicidal when he is told he has to retire after fifty years of teaching. He wonders if he made any impression on all on the many pupils who came and went over the decades. Professor Fowler will find the answer to that question in the Twilight Zone...

The Changing of the Guard is most notable for a beautiful performance from Donald Pleasance as the kind old teacher concerned about his legacy. "They come and go like ghosts. Faces, names, smiles, the funny things they said or the sad things, or the poignant ones. Poetry that left their minds the minute they themselves left. Aged slogans that were out of date when I taught them. I moved nobody. I motivated nobody."

The Changing of the Guard plays sort of like a ghostly Twilight Zone version of Dead Poet's Society and I love the winter bound anachronistic school. They had to put old age make-up on Pleasance to make him look like an old man but both he and the make-up are convincing enough to give the character authenticity. Pleasance apparently only had a few days to prepare for this role so his performance is all the more impressive.

The Changing of the Guard is touching episode and nicely directed. This is a lovely and moving story with a very chilly Christmas aura.

A CHARLIE BROWN CHRISTMAS (1965)

A Charlie Brown Christmas is an animated short which has become something of a beloved Christmas favourite in the United States. The premise of the film has Charlie Brown searching for the meaning of Christmas. Charlie Brown and Snoopy were created by Charles M. Schulz. Schulz infused much of his life into the long running newspaper comic strip adventures of Charlie and his colourful Beagle. Schulz was often an unhappy man who really did feel like an outsider despite his fame and wealth. He felt every romantic rejection or slight from his youth for years and years and was essentially Charlie Brown.

Both Charlie and his creator always seemed to have a nagging suspicion that everyone else was having a better time than them as they pursued a sometimes lonely quest for social acceptance. Charlie was Schulz's loner outsider neurotic side, Linus his eccentric oddball side, piano playing prodigy Schroeder his meticulous side, and Snoopy represented the side of him that gazed out of the window to dream. The female characters, by contrast, were based on women Schulz knew. The aggressive and loud Lucy is based on his headstrong first wife and mother and the 'little red-haired-girl' who Charlie is hopelessly besotted with from afar is based on Donna Mae Johnson, a young woman who Schulz loved from afar in the fifties.

Charlie Brown comics began life in the fifties as 'Li'l Folks' but the syndicate insisted on 'Peanuts', much to Schulz's irritation. Schulz's work was very radical in the medium when it first appeared. He wasn't afraid of empty white spaces in his panels and made his characters rudimentary but incredibly expressive. Comic strip sound bubbles like 'zap!' and 'pow!' were replaced by an understated sigh or resigned groan from Charlie. Schulz used six-year-old children to reflect the fears and troubles of adults (and himself) and even introduced themes like psychiatry, with Lucy's makeshift therapist stall often visited by Charlie Brown.

At first, Snoopy was a background character, just Charlie's eccentric dog, but Snoopy became as much the star of the strips as his master in the sixties, adding a surreal flourish to the Charlie Brown universe with his various canine capers, which included writing a novel, playing tennis, going on camping expeditions with Woodstock and feathered friends, battling the fearsome (but never seen) cat from next door, or merely sitting atop his kennel snoozing or pretending he's an ace fighter pilot.

Peanuts had a remarkably wide readership (300 million readers in 75 countries). College students and hippies loved it and Ronald Reagan was a fan too, once remarking that he always started his day by reading Charlie Brown in the newspaper. A flood of merchandising (I can distinctly remember having a Snoopy watch and lunch box when I was at primary school) poured forth from the cartoons, eventually putting Schulz up there with people like Oprah Winfrey in terms of his earnings as one of the richest entertainers in America.

A Charlie Brown Christmas is just a warm, amusing, festive, and very enjoyable cartoon. Charlie (a boy clearly ahead of his time!) is disheartened by the increasingly commercial nature of Christmas but agrees to direct a Christmas play in the hope that he might find some deeper meaning to the holiday. This is a really nice story because - just for once - all the kids (even Lucy) rally around Charlie to help him find comfort and happiness in Christmas. This film only runs to about half an hour so you have no excuse not to add it to your list of Christmas viewing entertainment.

A CHRISTMAS CAROL (1971)

This is an animated version of the Dickens tale and was directed by Richard Williams. It was made for ABC but actually got a theatrical release in the end and won the Academy Award for Best Animated Short Film. Alistair Sim reprises his role as Scrooge and there's another link to the 1951 live action classic because Michael Hordern is the voice of Marley's Ghost.

The film is beautifully narrated by Michael Redgrave and the other voice actors include Joan Sims and Diana Quick. Although this film only runs to about 25 minutes it still does an excellent job in adapting the story and the animation - although quite simple on the surface - is rather cinematic with zooms and shimmering ghostly spirits. The voice acting, as one would expect of such a cast, is terrific and the flashbacks as scrooge is taken on his ghostly journey are full of atmosphere and lovely country animations.

Perhaps the best thing of all about this animated film though is that it is also rather spooky for a cartoon. I suspect that children would be rather entranced by this film and find the slightly scary elements very enjoyable. This is definitely a Christmas Carol adaptation that deserves more exposure this days as it's a faithful and enjoyable animated rendition of the story with bags of atmosphere and a top notch voice cast. Given the fact that it runs to less than half an hour too you really have no reason not to make it part of your festive viewing plans.

A CHRISTMAS CAROL (1984)

Yet another version of A Christmas Carol? How many more of these do we need? Well, hold your horses for a moment because this one has the great George C. Scott playing Scrooge.

Scott was a highly acclaimed film actor but his career was somewhat on the way down by now and he was starting to take roles in television movies. This version of A Christmas Carol, directed by Clive Donner, is a very handsome production shot on location in England. It was a fantastically chilly but cosy ice glazed Victorian atmosphere.

There's a terrific cast too around Scott with David Warner as Bob Cratchit and Susannah York as Mrs Cratchit. Frank Finlay is Marley's Ghost, Angela Pleasence is the Spirit of Christmas Past, and Edward Woodward is the Spirit of Christmas Present. Look out too for Nigel Davenport as Silas Scrooge and Michael Gough as Mr Poole. There are a positive slew of acclaimed British thesps all over the place in this film.

Scott makes a great Scrooge too. Scott could be quite an explosive sort of actor (his performance in The Exorcist III is fantastic if you ask me - especially when his detective character loses his temper!) but he nicely underplays the part of Scrooge in this film and this makes the transformation of the character at the end all the more effective.

Scott makes Scrooge strangely realistic in this version and is different enough from others who have played this part (and an awful LOT of people have played Scrooge over the years) to make the role his own. The period trappings are beautifully done and some of the supernatural flourishes are even quite scary at times.

Sadly, this version of A Christmas Carol seems a trifle forgotten these days and rarely seems to appear on television. That's a great shame I think because it's a terrific television movie with excellent production values and a great cast. If you've never seen this before it is well worth tracking down.

A CHRISTMAS CAROL (1999)

This is a television version of Dickens' timeless story featuring Patrick Stewart as Scrooge. The film was directed by David Jones. The question with any new version of this story is whether or not it justifies its own existence. Do we really need yet ANOTHER version? Well, purely on the strength of Patrick Stewart's performance this version does justify its own existence and is certainly worth watching.

This is a bit darker and more brooding than other versions and Stewart's very controlled (if occasionally theatrical) performance works quite well. The film is well directed too and has a few nice flourishes which open it up somewhat - like the scenes involving ships at sea. Prior to this film Stewart had been performing a one man play based on A Christmas Carol where he played all the characters. He obviously doesn't do that in the movie but he's clearly got portraying Scrooge down a reasonably fine art after all that time on the stage.

Richard E. Grant is good here too as Bob Cratchit. I like the way Bob Cratchit is rather terrified of Scrooge at times! There are a smattering of fine supporting actors too like Dominic West and Liz Smith. This is as handsome as you'd expect a period rendition of this famous tale to be with excellent staging and plenty of atmosphere. The ghosts are actually quite scary too and add some enjoyable spookiness to the piece. Although most could be forgiven if we feel sometimes feel like there have been too many versions of this story you should certainly find the time to give this 1999 version a whirl if you've never done so before.

CHRISTMAS EVIL (1980)

Christmas Evil (aka You Better Watch Out) was written and directed by Lewis Jackson. Four years after this film came out a movie called Silent Night, Deadly Night created a rumpus by depicting a murderous killer dressed as Santa Claus. The thing is though that Christmas Evil had already done this but elicited no such controversy - presumably because so few people saw the film! Christmas Evil is a vastly superior film to Silent Night, Deadly Night too. Christmas Evil is more of a psychological drama than a horror film - though it does have some slasher elements in the second half. This is a morbidly compelling film which will linger in the memory long after you've seen it.

The story revolves around Harry Stadling (Brandon Maggart), a middle-aged man who works in a toy factory. Harry lives alone and the other workers at the factory think he's a bit of a loser. Harry is rather troubled by a strange memory from a childhood Christmas when his father dressed up as Santa. As an adult, Harry has an obsession with Father Christmas which you can only describe as deeply weird. Harry secretly spies on local children and keeps a log on whether they've been good or bad. He is dismayed by his colleagues at work because they don't really care about the toys they make or charity deeds in the community.

Harry, who is becoming dangerously disturbed, comes to believe that he is actually Santa Claus. So he dresses up as Santa, loads up a sack with presents, and goes off into the night in his van. He delivers gifts to children, dances at a Christmas party, and settles a few scores along the way. Suffice to say, Harry is now completely crazy.

Christmas Evil is a surprisingly effective film thanks mainly to the brilliant performance by Brandon Maggart as Harry. He has many memorable moments in the film. One of the most unforgettable comes when Harty tells some children that if they've been good they'll get presents every year but if they've been bad they'll get something 'horrible'. The intensity of this dialogue is completely compelling.

This is a decent looking film despite the low-budget with

streets blanketed in snow and elaborate Christmas lights. There's a great scene where Harry tries to climb down a chimney but gets stuck and has to pull himself back out again. Those expecting a slasher horror film will probably be disappointed but there are some rather grisly deaths at the back end of the film. There is just something morbidly entrancing about Christmas Evil. you just can't stop watching as Harry slides deeper and deeper down a rabbit hole of insanity as he drives around in his grubby Santa suit having these bizarre and often dark Christmas adventures.

The film is really well designed too. I like the way Harry's apartment has a big fluffy white carpet which gives the effect of snow. The supporting cast is pretty good too. Look out for Jeffrey DeMunn as Harry's concerned brother. DeMunn was later known for his association with Frank Darabont and played Dale in the early seasons of The Walking Dead. Christmas Evil loses its way a little at the end when a vigilante mob (complete with flaming torches!) chases Harry around the city but the ending is certainly memorable.
Christmas Evil is a bizarre experience quite unlike anything you'll encounter and all in all is a surprisingly decent little Christmas thriller.

A CHRISTMAS HORROR STORY (2015)

A Christmas Horror Story is an anthology horror film directed by Grant Harvey, Steven Hoban, and Brett Sullivan. This is a surprisingly decent effort and better than you probably expect it to be. The framing device is not bad either. It features William Shatner as a drunken DJ named Hoban doing a radio shift over Christmas. Holban keeps reporting on some sort of trouble going on down at the mall and warns his listeners to stay away from that place. The mall is later used for a nice twist at the end of the film when we finally see what this trouble was all about. Shatner's DJ pops up several times during the film as we weave in and out of the stories.

There are four distinct segments in the film but this is not a traditional horror anthology where we get the stories one after the other. We keep cross-cutting between them and they also overlap somewhat - with certain characters appearing in more than one of the jumbled up segments.

The first story has a group of students - Dylan (Shannon Kook), Ben (Alex Ozerov), and Molly Simon (Zoé De Grand Maison) - breaking into their school to investigate murders which occurred there in the past. The school has a supposedly dark history and used to be a convent. Well, as you might guess, these teenagers run into big trouble of the supernatural kind and are soon in great danger. This is the most familiar of the stories in the film and the sort of thing you feel like you've seen a million times in other horror films. How many horror films have been based around teenagers sneaking into some sort of building with a dark history? About 27 gazillion by my count. It's well made but this particular thread in the film is probably the least interesting.

The second story concerns Scott Peters (Adrian Holmes) - a police officer who we've already glimpsed in the first segment. With Christmas almost here, Scott takes his wife Kim (Oluniké Adeliyi) and son Will (Orion John) into the woods to chop down a Christmas tree. However, Will goes missing for a short time and when they find him and take him home it gradually becomes apparent that something dark has happened to him. He isn't the same person. This is a riff on the 'demon child' genre of horror and perfectly watchable for what it is. It isn't terribly original but it is well done.

The third story has a family of four heading out to the middle of a snow bound nowhere to visit their elderly Aunt Edda (Corrine Conley). They seem to be after an inheritance of some sort but things don't go well and they scurry off after being frightened by Edda's tales of Krampus - a mythological beast.

Well, as you might have guessed, the family then encounter Krampus. They end up trapped in a church and wonder if confessing their sins might save them. This segment is quite good fun and has a few twists near the end.

The last story is probably the best one. This has Santa Claus (George Buza) facing a crisis when his elves turn into zombies and conspire against him. Gruesome carnage follows as Santa battles these diminutive minions of the undead. This story is beautifully designed and shot and a lot of fun.

The film wraps up with a great twist which is satisfying enough to tie the anthology up with a bow and leave us happy. Despite not being a traditional anthology, the jumbling up of the stories in A Christmas Horror Story actually works relatively well. They give us little slithers of each tale and so they never threaten to outstay their welcome. This is not what you would describe as a classic anthology but it's not bad at all and a likeable effort with some decent acting and interesting stories.

A CHRISTMAS STORY (1983)

A Christmas story is a comedy film based on Jean Shepherd's semi-fictional anecdotes (primarily from his 1966 book In God We Trust: All Others Pay Cash). This film was directed by Bob Clark and has become a beloved Christmas staple in the United States. The film is basically a series of vignettes concerning young Ralphie Parker (Peter Billingsley) and his family in Hammond, Indiana. The film is narrated by the older Ralphie looking back on his childhood.

This is one of those films that is better just watched than described. It perfectly captures the strange, confusing, sometimes magical, sometimes frightening world of childhood and perhaps even Christmas too. This film is beautifully nostalgic and reminds me somewhat of that Woody Allen film Radio Days (which is also about someone looking back at their childhood and family). A Christmas Story has a rich period atmosphere and lashings of Christmas residue.

There are many memorable scenes in the film, like Ralphie being terrified by a department store Santa (this scene is shot from Ralphie's perspective and wonderfully done). This is a film that everyone can relate to in the way that it depicts Christmas as a strange but wonderful time where reality is happily banished for a few days. Who can forget too the scene where an enraged Ralphie turns on a bully who throws a snowball at his face?

Peter Billingsley is terrific as Ralphie and the depiction of his family life feels completely convincing. You really believe in these characters. If anyone steals the film though it is Darren McGavin as Ralphie's father. McGavin is wonderfully cranky and amusing in this film. One of the interesting things about this film is that it didn't do especially well when it came out and got fairly bog standard reviews. Over the decades though it has become a big cult classic and a film that many people like to watch at Christmas. It's just an amusing, enjoyable, and well made film with a fine cast. It fully deserves its cult status.

A CHRISTMAS TALE (2008)

A Christmas Tale (Un conte de Noël) is a French comedy-drama film directed by Arnaud Desplechin. The film is about the large Vuillard family gathering for Christmas. Junon Vuillard (Catherine Deneuve) is the matriarch of the family but she has something of a bombshell this Christmas because she reveals she is having treatment for a serious illness. As this eclectic gaggle of relatives meet up again there are tears, laughs, reflections on the past, and an attempt to repair and reflect on the various connections (or disconnections in some cases) that they share.

Your enjoyment of A Christmas Tale is probably going depend

on how much you like French films. In the tradition of French drama this film is talky, a trifle pretentious, and really long (A Christmas Tale goes on for about twenty minutes shy of three hours - which definitely feels TOO long in the end) but there are some great performances here and the complex and different relationships within a large family are explored in deft fashion.

This is not exactly Little Women in terms of Christmas spirit but it is set around Christmas and is essentially about how - for better or worse - Christmas is a time when relatives must usually come together. A Christmas Tale is about what happens very different people are forced to meet up again. Look out by the way for Mathieu Amalric as the black sheep of the Vuillard family. This same year, Amalric was the villain in the forgettable Bond film Quantum of Solace.

THE CROWDED DAY (1954)

The Crowded Day is a British film directed by John Guillermin. It was written by Talbot Rothwell - who would later write several Carry On films. The Crowded Day often plays like a whimsical comedy of the era but it does have elements of drama - including a character who is pregnant but unmarried (a [plot which made the film somewhat bold and risque for the time). The Crowded Day is about a group of women who work in a busy department store around Christmas. As a consequence of this the film has many Christmas trappings.

This is quite an unusual sort of British film for the era in that it provides a big showcase for a group of female actors. You do though get a nominal male lead in the reliable form of John Gregson. The Crowded Day has the bright and breezy appeal of other comedies of this era but the dramatic subplot gives it a bit more depth than your average British comedy. The life of this department store and the people who work there all feel authentic and the characters are all fairly vivid and have their own personalities.

There is an amazing cast here with a raft of familiar faces. Sid James, Thora Hird, Dandy Nichols, Prunella Scales (aka Mrs Basil Fawlty), Dora Bryan. The film was shot in a real department store and the ensemble of actors are excellent. The Crowded Day gives you a bit of everything really. Comedy, romance, heartbreak, drama. By the way, there is actually a theory that this movie was the inspiration for the popular 1970s sitcom Are You Being Served? One can certainly see the similarities at times between the too. The Crowded Day is probably not something that will linger in the memory for too long afterwards but you should should have a good time watching it all the same.

THE CURSE OF THE CAT PEOPLE (1944)

The Curse of the Cat People was directed by Robert wise and a sequel to the classic Val Lewton/Jacques Tourneur horror film Cat People. In the first film, Serbian émigré Irena Dubrovna (Simone Simon) attracts the attention of marine engineer Oliver Reed (Kent Smith) at the zoo after she discards some paper on which she was sketching a black panther. The pair have some tea together and become close - eventually marrying. However, Irene believes that she is cursed because of witchcraft in her old European village and that if she becomes intimate with her husband she will turn into a panther and place him in great harm.

This sequel, save for a few characters, doesn't have much in common with the first film and is more of a ghost story than anything but it is a very stylish film. This sequel takes place at Christmas and so has plenty of Christmas atmosphere. Snow, Christmas trees etc. The plot has Oliver Reed (Kent Smith), who married the doomed Irena in the first film, now remarried with a young daughter named Amy (Ann Carter).

Amy claims to have a friend that only she can see but it transpires that this imaginary friend is actually a vision of Irena. While you can never quite avoid the impression that this film is a very tenuous sort of sequel (it could easily have just been a completely unrelated film if they'd removed Kent Smith and Simone Simon) it's still a pretty good film in its own right and the story does at least supply a way for Simone Simon to come back.

The main character here is Reed's daughter Amy and Ann Carter (who was a prolific child actress of the era) is decent enough in this role. The Curse of the Cat People is a very dreamy sort of film and the appearances by Irena are beautifully designed and shot. In a sense, Irena is like a Guardian Angel in this film and that is a perfect match for the Christmas atmosphere. Look out by the way for that stunning blizzard scene. The Curse of the Cat People can't match the atmosphere and scares of the first film but it's a fairly solid and enjoyable attempt to do something different.

DEAD END (2003)

Dead End is a 2003 horror film written and directed by Jean-Baptiste Andrea and Fabrice Canepa. A bickering family, led by Frank Harrington (Ray Wise), are on the way to visit relatives on Christmas Eve. Frank decides to take a short cut but they end up on a long stretch of spooky forest road which never seems to end. They find a young woman in white (played by Amber Smith) wandering the road with her baby and from here things begin to become alarmingly strange. There seem to be strange voices in the woods, they are plagued by a black hearse, and one by one the Harrington family are stalked by an unfathomable supernatural presence.

Dead End is rather like an extra long episode of Rod Serling's Night Gallery with modern gore and effects. The family are quite annoying at first but the film is quick in cutting to the chase and plunging them all into a mysterious and nightmarish situation from which there seems to be no escape. It's a simple idea for a horror movie (family stuck on a dark stretch of road) but works very well and the film is both compelling and creepy. This is quite a crude and nasty film too so it definitely isn't for kids. It does though have plenty of Christmas references. The family even sing Christmas carols in the car in an attempt to pass the time.

The actors are good too with Ray Wise a solid anchor and Lin Shaye engagingly bonkers as his wife Laura. Alexandra Holden is also good as the daughter Marion. Marion is by far the most intelligent and logical member of the family and so - despite the fact she's as confused and terrified as anyone - she becomes the main character essentially. Dead End is shrewd in that there is no preamble to the strangeness and horror and it only runs to about 85 minutes so never outsays its welcome or stretches the premise beyond breaking point. On the whole this is a very watchable Christmas thriller only realy weakened by its slightly clunky ending.

DEADLY GAMES (1989)

Deadly Games (3615 code Père Noël) is a French film directed by René Manzor. The film's premise has an action movie obsessed kid named Thomas (Alain Lalanne) having to use all of his wits and ingenuity to fight off a deranged lunatic dressed as Santa Claus who has got inside the high-tech mansion where Thomas lives with his partially blind grandfather.

The director of this films claimed that Home Alone ripped off his movie and while it is true that they have a similar sort of premise, Home Alone is a cuddly family movie while Deadly Games is a 15 certificate thriller with much more of an edge.

This is a very inventive and well designed film that is more of a horror movie than anything despite some Amblin style Spielbergian flourishes. It's a reminder that the French film industry is perfectly capable of doing things besides angsty quirky family dramas set in Paris.

The kid is great and the film is always compelling. Demerits though for killing the dog. I hate it when films place animals in peril. Such a cheap device. Anyway, Deadly Games is sort of like a French version of something Tim Burton or Joe Dante might have done in their pomp but its has an energy and French style all of its own. If you are looking for some Christmas themed entertainment which is a trifle different from the norm then Deadly Games will supply that.

DEAD OF NIGHT (1945)

Dead of Night is a classic and highly influential 1945 British portmanteau horror film by Ealing Studios featuring stories directed by Alberto Cavalcanti, Charles Crichton, Basil Dearden and Robert Hamer. There is indeed a Christmas segment in this film - hence is inclusion in our list. The film begins with architect Walter Craig (Mervyn Johns) arriving at a country house where a number of guests are waiting. Walter immediately has a strange and powerful sense of deja vu and feels like he has been here in this same situation before. He explains, to a rather dubious audience, that each of them is part of a nightmare he is having and predicts an event that soon happens to try and prove his point. Everyone is soon intrigued, except for psychiatrist Dr Van Straaten (Frederick Valk). "Well, if I am a puppet and Mr Craig's pulling the strings, the least he can do is to tell me a little bit more about the part he's giving me to play," says the doctor. "I wish it were as easy as that," replies Walter. "But trying to remember a dream is like, how shall I put it, being out at night in a thunder-storm. There's a flash of lightning and, for one brief moment, everything stands out: vivid and startling."

We return to the country house and the various characters debating Walter's suggestion throughout the film and his confession induces them to talk about their own strange experiences. In horror anthology tradition we see the experiences they relate in the form of short stories all linked by the guests in the country house...

The first story - The Hearse Driver - was directed by Basil Dearden from a story by E. F. Benson. "Well, when it comes to foreseeing the future," says racing driver Hugh Gainger (Anthony Baird) to Dr Van Straaten in the country house. "Something once happened to me that knocks your theories into a cocked hat. Something I'll not forget to my dying day." In Hugh's story we begin with him recovering in hospital after a crash and the dapper sporting hero is soon charming his nurse. One night though, Hugh wakes up in the middle of night and decides to read a book for a while. He's rather perturbed to see daylight outside and, more worryingly, an anachronistic horse-drawn hearse and the driver (Miles Malleson) looking at him. "Just room for one inside, sir," says the hearse driver cheerfully to Hugh.

Grainger goes back to bed and eventually shrugs it off as a dream or delusion but, in this tale of premonition, the dream will come back to haunt him. Despite a simple and slight set-up, The Hearse Driver is expertly handled with a nice twist in the tale that will cause a few chills. Dead of Night has a nice offbeat and supernatural air throughout - a sort of film within a dream feeling - and The Hearse Driver is a good example of this.

The next story is The Christmas Story and was directed by Alberto Cavalcanti. At a Christmas party in an old spacious house, young Sally (Sally Ann Howes) plays hide and seek and has a nice time but an obstreperous scamp enjoys telling Sally that the house is haunted because of an old murder that occurred way back in 1860. Sally later stumbles across a sobbing boy at the top of a hidden flight of stairs (which will soon be disconcertingly elusive) who tells her that unspeakable threats are being made to him. She consoles the boy and returns to the party but Sally is about to get a very unsettling surprise. A ridiculously simple premise is used to wonderfully eerie effect in this story with the black and white adding to the weird and wonderfully anachronistic atmosphere. Though a little mawkish at times, this story is fantastically ghostly and British and does have a suitably spooky twist that is very creepy.

The next tale is The Haunted Mirror, directed by Robert Hamer from a story by John V. Baines. Joan (Googie Withers) buys a Victorian mirror from an antique shop for her fiance Peter (Ralph Michael) but when Peter uses the mirror he has a vague impression that the reflection he sees doesn't match his own surroundings and eventually becomes withdrawn and bad tempered. The 'visions' are starting to affect Peter greatly and when Joan forces him to look in the mirror with her he sees a strange Victorian scene and an ornate bedroom with a log fire. "But in a queer sort of way, it fascinates me," says Peter of the mirror. "I feel as though that room, the one in the mirror, were trying to... to claim me. To draw me into it. It almost becomes the real room, and my own bedroom imaginary." Joan naturally suspects her fiance might be going completely mad but a visit to the antique shop reveals the true origin and secret of the mirror.

A strong segment and clearly an influence on similar spooky mirror shenanigans with David Warner in the seventies Amicus compendium From Beyond the Grave. This story pulls you in as things become ever more strange and Ralph Michael does a decent job as the spooky reflections in the mirror eventually begin to threaten Peter's sanity.

The next offering is The Golfing Story directed by Charles Crichton. It stars Basil Radford and Naunton Wayne as rival golfers George and Larry, forever feuding on the golf course but otherwise good friends. George and Larry's friendship is threatened however when Mary (Peggy Bryan) can't choose between them. They decide, as you do, to play eighteen holes of golf for her, with the loser to be a decent chap and disappear... permanently. "The loser to vanish from the scene," says George. The triumphant George wins the prize but will Larry let him enjoy it?

Perhaps the weakest link in the film, The Golfing Story is a fairly jovial jape and seems a tad out of place in the film as a whole but it is quite likeable nonetheless and serves as a sort of spoof of glossy 'afterlife' films. It's quite amusing at times ("Cheat! Cad! Twister! May the Lord have mercy on your handicap!") and the set-up, play golf, loser commits suicide, is fairly dark despite the whimsical nature of the piece.

The final and most famous story in Dead of Night is The Ventriloquist's Dummy, directed by Cavalcanti again and featuring Michael Redgrave as nutty ventriloquist Maxwell Frere.

Maxwell's major problem is that he is becoming increasing dominated by his dummy Hugo which is, it has to be said, a bit scary and not the most pleasant character. Under the growing influence of this creepy puppet, things are only going to go from bad to worse for Maxwell.

The Ventriloquist's Dummy has been done subsequent times since Dead of Night came out, from Magic with Anthony Hopkins to Child's Play, but the copycats have yet to diminish the more vintage chills supplied here. Michael Redgrave is really good in this segment as the nervous, twitchy ventriloquist rapidly heading for a nervous breakdown and there is a scary final scene to wrap things up. I like too the depiction of a certain boozy low-rent post-war showbusiness world where people are struggling to get by as the country tries to get back on its feet again. This story is very creepy and there are some genuinely unsettling moments, especially when Hugo suddenly starts talking to American ventriloquist Sylvester Kee (Hartley Power) without Maxwell or we get the warning "You don't know what Hugo's capable of..."

We then return to the country house and the final wrap-up which is very eerie, incorporating all the stories and continuing the dreamlike atmosphere of the film. The country house banter is good fun on the whole and contains all the characters. I should mention Roland Culver as Eliot Foley, the man who invited them in the first place, who is good value debating with Craig and Van Straaten. Dead of Night is made to feel like a recurring nightmare and the black and white and post-war detail and atmosphere adds a great deal to the ghostly trappings. If you suspect that a British black and white film made way back in 1945 is unlikely to supply any chills today then Dead of Night will prove you wrong. One to watch late at night with the lights off.

DEADPOOL (2016)

Yes, Deadpool makes it onto our list by virtue of a Christmas scene in a montage! Created by artist/writer Rob Liefeld and writer Fabian Nicieza, Deadpool first appeared in The New Mutants #98 (cover-dated February 1991). Initially Deadpool was depicted as a supervillain when he made his first appearance in The New Mutants and later in issues of X-Force, but later evolved into his more recognizable antiheroic persona.

Deadpool is a disfigured and mentally unstable mercenary with the superhuman ability of an accelerated healing factor and physical prowess. He is known as the "Merc with a Mouth" because of his talkative nature and tendency to break the fourth wall, which is used by writers for humorous effect and running gags.

Ryan Reynolds played a version of Deadpool in X-Men Origins: Wolverine but wanted to try the character again in a more faithful way to the source material. So this new Deadpool film was fashioned almost as an experimental superhero film that would be more adult, violent, postmodern and risque than your standard Marvel fare. The tactic worked when Deadpool garnished good reviews and - unbelievably - made as much money as the much more expensive Batman v Superman. The film is presented in a nonlinear narrative. Wade Wilson (Reynolds), a former special forces operative working as a mercenary, meets an escort named Vanessa at a local bar. The initial meeting evolves into a relationship. A year later, Wilson proposes to her, but he is then diagnosed with liver, lung, prostate, and brain cancer. Despite Vanessa's love, Wilson detests the thought of her watching him waste away, and he leaves her in the middle of the night.

A recruiter from a covert organization approaches Wilson and promises him abilities that will cure his cancer. Wilson reluctantly agrees. He is taken to a remote laboratory where he meets Ajax (Ed Skrein) and Angel Dust (Gina Carano), and instantly resents them. Ajax injects a mutation-activating serum into Wilson and subjects him to daily torture to activate it.

When Wilson's body fails to respond, Ajax asphyxiates him in an oxygen chamber, causing him to develop an accelerated healing factor that cures him but leaves him disfigured with burn like scars over his entire body. Wilson finds a way to destroy the lab and escapes his confines. He is now obsessed with finding Ajax to seek revenge and a cure. Deadpool is a refreshing antidote for those who feel that the superhero genre has become too samey and predictable. The fairly small scale action packs a punch and Ryan Reynolds, usually the most irritating of actors, is given funny lines. Naturally he breaks the fourth wall and trashes Green Lantern amongst other targets.

Even the love story works well and consequently Deadpool keeps our engagement with these characters and makes us care about them. No small feat given how Deadpool behaves in the film. Stefan Kapicic as Colossus and Brianna Hildebrand as Negasonic Teenage Warhead are nice additions too. There's a funny bit where Deadpool comments that it's strange how they always seem to be the only two people in when he goes to the X-Men's mansion. Almost as if the film could only afford two X-Men! Deadpool is entertaining and witty and at a fraction of the budget puts 2016 superhero films like Batman v Superman to shame.

THE DEVIL OF CHRISTMAS (2016)

This is an episode of the enjoyable anthology show Inside No.9 created by Reece Shearsmith and Steve Pemberton. The Devil of Christmas was originally broadcast as a special Christmas episode on the 27th of December 2016. This episode features the Krampus legend. In Central European folklore, Krampus is a horned, anthropomorphic figure described as half-goat and half-demon who, during the Christmas season, punishes children who have misbehaved.

It is Christmas 1977. A family of Julian (Pemberton), wife Kathy (Jessica Raine), son Toby (George Bedford), and mother Celia (Rula Lenska), travel to an Austrian chalet where they are told the terrifying story of Krampus by the guide Klaus (Shearsmith). Strange things soon start to happen.

This episode is sort of a film within a film. The Devil of Christmas is a fictional film/tv episode and the director (voiced by Derek Jacobi) tells us about its production as we watch and listen in the form of what seems to be an audio commentary. However, this being Inside No. 9, all is not quite what it seems.

The Devil of Christmas is - with the possible exception of the Halloween special Dead Line - the most successful of Inside No. 9's horror episodes and a very entertaining and amusing piece of television. The recreation of a vintage seventies anthology episode is not exactly realistic (despite the clever technical way that the look of television from the seventies is replicated, the film we see in this episode always feels more of a spoof than an authentic piece of mimicry!) but it is an awful lot of fun.

This episode feels rather like an amusing parody at times of the way that television in the seventies would cut corners in a very obvious way. When characters from something like, for example, Whatever Happened to the Likely Lads?, were supposed to be abroad they were always quite patently in a small studio set in England pretending to be in Switzerland or something with a fake painting depicting the view outside of their window of ski slopes and mountains. The Devil of Christmas really taps into that era of bargain basement television production.

What really makes The Devil of Christmas work too is that the fact that we find ourselves becoming quite engrossed in the Krampus mystery at the heart of the story the actors are appearing in. The mysterious Klaus fills their heads with tales of the dreaded Krampus and strange things soon start to happen. Is the legend of Krampus really going to make an appearance?

Derek Jacobi is entertaining throughout as the narrator in The Devil of Christmas. His narrating director Dennis Fulcher occasionally interjects to pedantically point out a continuity error or (less pedantically and more understandably) highlight some terrible acting from a member of the cast. He mutters his random thoughts in much the way that someone would in a real audio commentary. 'I very nearly didn't do this film. But there was so little work around I felt I couldn't say no. The week before I'd had a meeting about Worzel Gummidge, but Pertwee had his favourites, I knew that from Who.'

This episode rather anticipates Dead Line in a way with the vague 'film within a film' structure. We didn't get to see much of the (sound problem plagued!) mystery in Dead Line but in The Devil of Christmas we get to watch the horror mystery that

Derek Jacobi's director is commenting on - and very enjoyable it is too.

The biggest praise you can give this episode is that the seasonal chiller we are watching is so entertaining it would have sufficed on its own even without the audio commentary device. The narration is like the icing on the cake though as it makes the episode even more enjoyable and is a crucial component of the shocking twist which awaits us at the conclusion.

The garish bright colours and dodgy acting are all part of the kitsch fun in The Devil of Christmas. Pemberton in particular is great as the ham actor trying to rattle through his shooting commitments as quickly as possible. He is given a preposterous mustache too. All of the cast here are good - as one has come to expect from Inside No. 9. Shearsmith makes the most of a more sinister and ambiguous part as Klaus and Lenska and Raine are both very good too.

There's a twist in the 'film within a film' but then another twist that takes us completely by surprise. This is probably the darkest twist that Inside No. 9 has ever attempted up to this point. This macabre and shocking (not to mention improbable but then this is the sort of twist that probably shouldn't be scrutinised too long for logic) ending more than lives up to the 'dark comedy with a twist' promise of Inside No. 9.

The expert blending of comedy and horror in The Devil of Christmas is Shearsmith and Pemberton at their best. We are almost lulled into this comic horror episode to the point where it becomes cosy and then - suddenly - are faced with the bleakest moment of horror imaginable. It really gives the coda a sense of impact and all is then revealed about the narration we have been listening to over the course of the story.

The Devil of Christmas is classic Shearsmith and Pemberton and one of the most memorable episodes of Inside No. 9. This episode is both funny and (then ultimately) shocking. It's another wonderful illustration of how Inside No. 9 can turn into a full blown straight horror show just when you least expect it. "It's all the more shocking when horror is hidden in a comedy," said Shearsmith of Inside No. 9. "People are sitting down to watch it in the same slot that they'd watch Open All Hours or Mrs Brown's Boys, and they're not geared up the way that they might be at 9 o'clock for a drama. So I think the punch is even more powerful."

There really isn't too much to complain about in The Devil of Christmas. The recreation of seventies television is clever and amusing, Shearsmith and Pemberton are both given fun characters to play, the supporting cast is great, and the episode well and truly whips the rug out from underneath you right at the end. In any discussion of the best episodes of Inside No. 9 you'd certainly have to give The Devil of Christmas a mention.

This is one of the best examples of the way that Inside No. 9 can combine comedy and horror without diluting the latter in the slightest. The last scene in The Devil of Christmas - rather like the end of The Harrowing - doesn't pull any punches at all in the horror stakes. It is arguably the darkest and bleakest moment in any episode of Inside No. 9 and - given the competition - that's really saying something!

DIE HARD (1988)

John McTiernan's film Die Hard takes place on Christmas Eve in Los Angeles. John McClane (Bruce Willis) is a New York policeman who has just flown into town to see his estranged wife Holly and their two children. Holly is at her company's Christmas party high in the Nakatomi Plaza - a glittering high-tech skyscraper. McClane eventually finds Holly at the party but - while he is freshening up in the bathroom - a group of highly sophisticated German terrorist thieves, led by super suave classic villain Hans Gruber, gatecrash the party and take complete control of the building and everyone hostage.

Their target is the $600 million in negotiable bearer bonds stashed in the apparently impenetrable vault of the Plaza and they will stop at nothing to get the money. As their elaborate plans are set in motion they gradually become aware that McClane, in a vest!, is loose in the skyscraper and doing everything he can to foil their brilliant scheme. A deadly game of cat and mouse begins...

The first trailers for Die Hard were met with some derision when they first appeared in America. Bruce Willis seemed a very unlikely actor to gatecrash the eighties Stallone/Schwarzenegger action scene and his huge fee for Die Hard was regarded to be somewhat ridiculous. He was the television actor from the funky postmodern romantic comedy series Moonlighting and considered far too big for his boots. If Die Hard was a flop it might have been back to television.

The greatest strength of Willis though was that he could be funny and knew how to deliver a quip. This quality served him well in Die Hard and the fact that he was a fairly Ordinary Joe was also an asset. Where Schwarzenegger was essentially indestructible, Willis gave us a different type of action hero. McClane was not superhuman but a more plausible, vulnerable hero who bleeds, gets beat up, makes mistakes, wisecracks ("Nine million terrorists in the world and I got to kill one with feet smaller than my sister!"), sometimes seems out of his depth, but ultimately triumphs because of sheer determination.

We root for John McClane because he's a down to earth blue collar screen hero. In the capable hands of John McTiernan, Die Hard was the most inventive and crowd-pleasing actioner for years and catapulted Willis to stardom. Every hero needs a good villain and they don't come much better than Hans Gruber. Alan Rickman is gloriously camp and great fun as Gruber, presenting a masterclass to any actor who wants to be a memorable baddie. He is overstated, understated, suave, sarcastic, chilling, funny, wonderfully urbane and polished, and even has a Bond style henchman in the unhinged Karl

Vreski who becomes obsessed with killing McClane for reasons
which will be understandable when you watch the film.
It's a joy to watch Rickman's performance as he makes the
most of a clever and funny script. "I am an exceptional thief,
Mrs McClane. And since I'm moving up to kidnapping, you
should be more polite!" Gruber is established early as a
cultured villain as he smoothly attempts to prise the code to
the vault from the Nakatomi boss Mr Takagi near the start of
the film. This scene also establishes that he's completely
ruthless when he doesn't get what he wants. It adds some
tension to a later scene where Hart Bochner as a drug addled
yuppie employee unwisely attempts to negotiate with Gruber.

Best bits? McClane riding on top of elevators and navigating
crawlspaces ("Now I know what a tv dinner feels like!") and
the SWAT team assault on the Nakatomi Plaza which leads to
some spectacular action scenes and explosions. Rarely have
explosions and destruction been so lovingly and strikingly shot
in a film. Willis rode on top of elevators for real in some
sequences and the moment where McClane misses one of the
crawlspaces and tumbles further down the elevator shaft
before managing to grab onto one was a mistake by a
stuntman that they kept in the film because they thought it
looked good.

There is a really funny moment where John McClane is on the
roof at night with a walkie talkie surrounded by the twinkling
sprawling lights of the city and trying to persuade a police line
that he's serious about the building being taken over and
losing his temper when a voice calmly tells him the line is only
for emergencies.

The film makes excellent use of Beethoven's 9th Symphony as
Gruber attempts to crack the Plaza's high-tech safe (the final
cracking of the vault is beautifully choreographed) and just
when you think Die Hard has reached a peak it hits the viewer
with a fresh wave of spectacular action, keeping the whole film
rattling along. There is a truly incredible scene where McClane
jumps off the top of the roof with a fire hose strapped to him

leading to a classic cliffhanger moment.

I also love McClane and Gruber meeting at last, another scene with a fine slab of tension. This 'Bill Clay' scene was written into the film when Alan Rickman was goofing around doing an American accent on the set. Steven E. de Souza and John McTiernan had been looking for a way to get a face to face meeting between Gruber and McClane into the story - as opposed to them only meeting at the end - and this gave them the idea of Gruber running into McClane while looking for his explosives and pretending to be an escaped hostage. Rickman and Willis improvised the dialogue to given it a spontaneous feel.

The police helicopters sweeping over the streets towards the skyscraper make for a spectacular sequence in the film - all the more impressive because John McTiernan had a limited amount of time to shoot the helicopter scenes. With the tragic Twilight Zone: The Movie accident (where actor Vic morrow and two child extras were killed when a helicopter got too low crashed onto them whilst shooting the John Landis segment) still fresh in the memory, McTiernan got nervous about safety and cancelled the last two helicopter runs for the roof sequence.

Note too how seamlessly McTiernan will interweave two different narratives so we have two simultaneous sequences in parallel. It's a device that many action films try to do but it somehow never quite has the same natural flow that McTiernan achieves here. The movement of the camera is key in the constricted environment of the film. We really feel like we are there following McClane around in the thick of the action and a few tilted angled camera shots add a nice off-kilter feel.

Shoot-outs result in ridiculous amounts of smashed glass which a barefoot McClane must negotiate! Bruce Willis wore special rubber shoes made to look like barefeet for this sequence. The moment where McClane picks a large shard of glass out of his foot in the bathroom is still liable to make you wince. The only scene the film could probably do without is a slightly mawkish bit where Willis gets a bit sentimental and dewy-eyed on the phone to Powell talking about his wife. It's his 'actor' moment but maybe he deserves it.

Though the action is firmly set in the Plaza, Die Hard has a large group of supporting characters that are often fun. Reginald VelJohnson is likeable as Sgt Al Powell, McClane's contact with the outside. In a nice twist Die Hard is almost a 'buddy film' where the friends aren't together at all. Paul Gleason is very funny as comically dim Deputy Police Chief Dwayne T Robinson and I love VelJohnson's Oliver Hardy style looks of disbelief at him whenever he says something idiotic. Gleason has a lot of funny lines.

Bonnie Bedelia is believable and tough as Holly and Robert Davi and Grand L Bush make a good comic team as two laconic gung-ho FBI Agents with the same surname. William Atherton is also good as sleazy journalist Richard Thornburg, out for a scoop after hearing about the crisis on a police frequency.

This character and the media bits just verge on the edge taking us out of the action too much but it's a minor quibble overall. Thornburg does play a part in the internal action though and supplies a big laugh at the end of the film. De'voreaux White is fun too as Argyle, a limo driver who ends up involved in the crisis after driving McClane to the Plaza from the airport. Gruber's gang are also well cast and a good bunch of film heavies.

Most of the villains in the film were not German in real life and so a lot of the German spoken in the film is complete gibberish! Gruber and his men had their names changed to suggest another nationality when the film was released in Germany as the government there felt that German terrorists/radicals, even in an action thriller like Die Hard, were still too sensitive an issue and might be in poor taste.

The most unique thing about the film though is the location.
Die Hard has a largely confined setting and is an incredibly
inventive film within this space. The Nakatomi Plaza (the
newly built corporate headquarters of 20th Century Fox was
used for exterior shots) is almost like an extra character in the
film and looks amazing under the production design of Jack
DeGovia. The film is also exceptionally well edited and John
McTiernan's only action peer around this time was James
Cameron. Die Hard is an involving crowd-pleaser with
spectacular set-pieces, tension, some good laughs and great
characters. It might just be the greatest action film ever made.

DIE HARD 2 (1990)

In Renny Harlin's Die Hard sequel, once again it is Christmas
Eve, two years after the Nakatomi Plaza caper, and John
McClane (wearing a blue checked shirt but you do get some
vague vest action) is at Dulles International Airport in
Washington waiting for his wife Holly to land. He doesn't
seem to ever have much luck at Christmas though because
once again he is soon up to his neck in trouble. A team of
mercenary terrorists, led by the renegade Colonel Stuart, seize
the airport by taking control of the air traffic control systems.
Stuart wants to rescue Ramon Esperanza, the drug baron
dictator of (the fictitious) Latin American country Val Verde.

Esperanza is due to fly in to stand trial and Stuart demands a
Boeing 747 to be put at his disposal to make his escape with
the dictator and his team. If his demands are not met he will
start crashing planes. As his wife is on one of those planes
(now circling the airport with its fuel running low) McClane
decides he has no choice but to take matters into his own
hands and try and wrest control of the airport back from
Stuart and his men...

One immediate problem with Die Hard 2 (sometimes known
as Die Hard 2: Die Harder on posters but not in the actual

titles!) is that the action is no longer wonderfully self-contained in the manner of the original. The constrictive setting of the shimmering skyscraper forced them to be more inventive and was a major part of the appeal.

Here they have an entire airport and its surroundings to play with and the novelty is unavoidably lost - making this seem much more like a generic action film than the first one. There is even a snowmobile chase at one point and while everyone loves a good snowmobile chase it does feel more like James Bond than the John McClane character we saw in the first film. The idea here is that if the first film was riffing on The Towering Inferno then this is Die Hard meets Airport but the setting and story simply doesn't work so well this time.

Years later, Bruce Willis expressed some dissatisfaction with Die Hard 2 when he was doing a press junket for Live Free or Die Hard. "Die Hard 2, because it came out so soon after the first film — the first film is so well built, and so well crafted and so claustrophobic, and the good guys and the bad guys and the hostages are all in one building, it's almost a perfect action scenario– the second film was kind of everywhere, we were all over the place. In retrospect I didn't like the fact that the second film was so self-referential to the first film."

McClane was somehow more realistic in the first film too, a reluctant hero. While he has an obvious motivation to intervene here (his wife is on one of the planes circling above) you do get the impression he'd do so anyway. It's highly contrived the manner in which he becomes suspicious of two military types at the start of the film and is soon having a guns blazing shoot out and scrap with them in some baggage room, thus stumbling onto Stuart's grand scheme for the first time.

No one can deny though that Die Hard 2 is a big film that gives you plenty of bang for your buck, gun fights lovingly framed and staged, explosions a plenty, spectacular sequences involving aeroplanes. It's a perfectly competent and entertaining action film but one that just feels somewhat functional and uninspired when placed alongside its illustrious predecessor. It's as if they were desperate to get another film with the Die Hard tag out as soon as possible rather than wait for anyone to come up with a really great idea or script.

Renny Harlin was fine at this sort of stuff and directed some good action films (Cliffhanger, The Long Kiss Goodnight) in his day but he lacks the refinement and panache of John McTiernan. Die Hard 2 throws a lot of money at the screen but is significantly less stylish and sleek than McTiernan's film and never generates that rush laden rollercoaster ride - that spectacular coda upon coda feeling. The first film had a vivid palette and sheen and this one is very blue and dark at times with a lot of action taking place at night. The fake dusty snow that frames proceedings doesn't always convince either.

The biggest problem with the film is probably William Sadler's villain - a bland and largely charisma free baddie who you can barely remember after watching the film. The camp thesping antics of Rickman and Jeremy Irons in the first and third films were much more fun and gave Willis more opportunity for verbal sparring. Gruber was witty, flamboyant and amusing but Sadler is no fun at all and seems like he's just wandered in from a Steven Segal film.

McClane's cat and mouse game with the other villains was much more inventive and enjoyable. Hans Gruber's domain was a high-tech skyscraper that he had complete control of like a king but Sadler and his men set up a HQ in a windblown shed in the airport grounds. It's not the same really.

As usual, McClane has to battle the authorities as much as the villains - especially the chief of airport security Captain Carmine Lorenzo. Fans of Hill Street Blues and NYPD Blue will enjoy the diminutive walrus mustached presence of Dennis Franz as Lorenzo. In a radical departure from his usual parts he essays a diminutive bad tempered walrus mustached policeman here! I love Dennis Franz so I was happy to see him.

The film lacks the wit of the first one and Willis only gets a few good wisecracks and laughs from the script (and his improvised gags) so his verbal jousts with Franz are sorely needed. "Hey Lorenzo, let me ask you something: what sets off a metal detector first? The lead in your ass or the s*** in your brains?" Willis throws himself into the action in his usual fashion and proves that he has more than enough charisma to carry a Die Hard picture on his shoulders without Alan Rickman in support. He'd arrived as a major film star.

One welcome thing about the film - that at least makes it seem like a blood relative to the first Die Hard - is the inclusion of some of the key supporting characters from the original. It's contrived of course but nice anyway to see these characters again.

Die Hard 2 is a lavish and generally entertaining film but one that perhaps does seem as if it is going through the motions rather than ever creating anything special or new with the franchise. It's watchable but tends to wash over you rather than leave a litter of unforgettable scenes and images in the memory as the first picture does. If this had been the first Die Hard film it's doubtful the brand would have become so iconic. Still, despite feeling more mechanical than Die Hard (you can almost hear Die Hard 2 desperately grinding through the gears) this is an expensive sequel that remains very watchable. It has some grand scale stunts and some solid laughs.

EDWARD SCISSORHANDS (1990)

Edward Scissorhands was directed by Tim Burton. You could argue that this is Burton's second best film after Ed Wood. The film conderns a strange young man (Johnny depp) found living alone in a Gothic mansion by an Avon saleslady Peg (played by Dianne Wiest). Edward was created by an inventor

(Vincent Price) but the inventor died before giving Edward hands - he has scissors for hands instead. Peg takes Edward back to her suburban home but Edward turns out to be a fish out of water in the real world. He falls in love with Peg's daughter Kim (Winona Ryder) but this invokes the wrath of Kim's macho boyfriend Jim (Anthony Michael Hall).

Edward Scissorhands is beautifully framed as if we are hearing a fairytale and takes place at Christmas. The most affecting scenes in the film come when Edward carves ice sculptures of Kim at rapid speed - the chips of ice flying into the air as he furiously carves away and giving the effect of snow. There's a great cast here and Depp is great as the bewildered Edward. Depp essentially has to give a silent film performance here as Edward is obviously not much of a talker. It is of course absolutely wonderful too to see Vincent Price here in what turned out to be his last film.

Edward Scissorhands is one of the most personal of Burton's films and he has obviously invested a lot of himself in the title character, that sense of being a complete outsider who struggles to fit into the ordinary world. Truth be told though the surburbia here is not exactly ordinary and depicted in a somewhat quirky way though. Edward Scissorhands has plenty of Christmas themed scenes and backdrops and is a lovely film on the whole. Be warned though this is a very bittersweet sort of film and not one of those Hollywood movies determined to shoehorn in a happy ending. As far as Edward Scissorhands goes though this feels rather apt and in tone with the mood of the story. The music by Danny Elfman is the perfect sonic backdrop for this touching and magical film.

ELF (2003)

Elf is a 2003 comedy film directed by Jon Favreau. Will Ferrell plays Buddy, a human who climbed into Santa's sack as a baby and was raised by elves. Despite his very human proportions,

Buddy presumes himself to be an elf. He learns that his biological father Walter Hobbs (James Caan) is a book publisher in New York but something of an old Scrooge. Buddy goes on a mission to meet Walter and change his ways but he predictably turns out to be a fish out of water in the human world to say the least.

Elf is one of those films that could easily have fallen flat or been a disaster but it actually works fairly well thanks mostly to Will Ferrel. Ferrell runs with the preposterous concept of the film and his spirited comic performance manages to carry the picture through some occasional lulls. There a nice supporting cast here too with Mary Steenburgen, Ed Asner, and James Caan. It's really Ferrel though who has to make this film work. If they'd miscast the lead this movie could have been a complete misfire.

It all builds to a fairly predictable last act but you should have fun getting there and the film has enough laughs to satisfy most viewers. This is a nice Christas film in that both kids and adults should find that it passes the time in fairly light and breezy fashion. You wouldn't quite say that Elf is a classic but it's definitely one of the more memorable Christmas comedies in (fairly) recent memory.

EMMA (2009)

This a BBC adaptation of the Jane Austen novel with Romola Garai as Emma Woodhouse. This has a rich festive atmosphere at times because there are scenes set on both Christmas Eve and Christmas Day. Jane Austen's story was first published in 1815 and concerns the title character - a young woman of utmost confidence. Emma is pretty sure she will never get married herself but that doesn't stop her from taking up the self-anointed role of the local matchmaker to get other people married. Emma is convinced that she was born to play his role and considers herself to be an expert on who should get married and who shouldn't. But does she have an over inflated view of her matchmaking abilities and could cupid's arrow yet strike her own heart?

Austen confessed that Emma was a heroine who is hard to like and this is certainly true to a point. Emma does, at first, seemed spoiled (she seems to live a life of pure leisure) and far too sure of herself. However, over the course of the story we see that Emma is also kind and patient (especially ith her father) and a much more complex character than she might seem at first glance.

You could say that the novel is quite an interesting experiment on the part of the author then in presenting a heroine who is flawed and human. The story remains strangely topical today as most people will have met a few people like Emma in their life. Someone who is very sure of themselves and thinks they know what is best for everyone else. The question though is what will be best for Emma. She will have to learn more about herself through the course of the story. The story still works as an amusing and artful satire of class and society. One big reason, besides the Christmas trappings, why you should watch this version too is the excellent support by Michael Gambon as Emma's father.

EYES WIDE SHUT (1999)

Eyes Wide Shut was based on Arthur Schnitzler's 1926 novella Traumnovelle (or Dream Story) and proved to be Stanley Kubrick's last ever film - its release posthumous. And yes, Eyes Wide Shut is definitely a Christmas film! There hadn't been a new Kubrick film for twelve years at the time and when word filtered out that Eyes Wide Shut was going to be a daring erotic thriller starring real life husband and wife Tom Cruise and Nicole Kidman, expectation and anticipation were relatively high. The end result - as usual - met with a mixed reception.

However, while earlier Kubrick films found their status and reputation increasing year on year the same is not true of Eyes Wide Shut. Eyes Wide Shut is not regarded to be one of the great Kubrick films or a cult classic. If anything, it's one of the Kubrick films that no one even remembers or have never seen. While Kubrick loyalists (including Martin Scorcese) maintain that Eyes Wide Shut is a great film, the general perception is that it's an interesting picture but not one that approaches his best work. Rather like later Roman Polanski films. Frantic. The Ninth Gate. The Ghost Writer. Very watchable and competent but not a patch on Chinatown or Rosemary's Baby.

The film mostly revolves around Dr Bill Harford (Tom Cruise). Harford has made a good living as physician to some wealthy clients and lives in a swanky upscale New York apartment with wife Alice (Nicole Kidman) and their young daughter. The film begins with them about to attend a Christmas bash hosted by Bill's friend Victor Ziegler (Sydney Pollack).

At the party, Alice is propositioned by a suave European bloke while Bill becomes the target of two models looking for a tryst. They want to take him to the end of the rainbow apparently. Neither encounter goes beyond flirting but it makes them both question fidelity and infidelity, even on a purely imaginary level.

Alice (under the influence of marijuana) becomes piqued when Bill declares at the next day later that he knows she would never cheat on him. Woman are faithful he says. Alice, irritated by his lack of interest or jealously in the thought of other men being attracted to her, announces that she once nearly cheated on him purely out of lust. Bill is mentally devastated by this bombshell and called away on an urgent medical emergency. Later, he walks the streets and gradually becomes drawn into a nether world of prostitutes and strange costumed gothic orgies organised by rich and mysterious people.

Eyes Wide Shut sounds more interesting than it ultimately

proves to be. Despite the hype the film is neither shocking, erotic or a thriller. It's a meditation on sex, power and money, how people live with the knowledge that they have no insight or control over the inner life/mind of even those closest to them. The recurring motifs here are the dehumanising of society and the individual and mirrors. Lots of mirrors. The orgy scenes are a bit risible at times (whenever I'm presented with gothic cult groups and secret societies I unavoidably start thinking of Hammer House of Horror or something and find it hard to take seriously) and when Tom Cruise was rumbled and asked for a second secret password at one of these parties I was unfortunately reminded of a scene in the Marx Brothers classic Horse Feathers where Groucho has to supply the right password to bootlegger Chico to enter a bar. "Swordfish!"

The general story is watchable enough. New York looks beautiful here at times. Maybe too beautiful, like in a romantic Woody Allen flm. Harford's debauched adventures strain credibility somewhat but the look of the film almost suggests this is some sort of dream state (I believe the novel veered towards this structure) although that might just be Stanley Kubrick. As you would expect every single frame of the film looks as if it was planned for years. Long tracking shots, the camera constantly moving, Kubrickian colour schemes. More red. Even Sydney Pollack's billiard table is red!

The big question here is can Tom Cruise carry the film and make you take it seriously? The answer is yes and no. He does well at times but then at other times you are always just aware that this is Tom Cruise doing a turn in a Kubrick film. He never completely loses himself in the character and makes you forget who he is. I do struggle to take Cruise seriously in dramatic roles. I think he's more of a star in popcorn fare than a serious actor despite the good work he has done in films like Rain Man and (maybe) Magnolia.

One problem with Cruise here is that he always looks about fifteen years old with his spookily youthful looks and diminutive stature. He's hard to take seriously sometimes in dramatic films. Nicole Kidman is better as Alice and more convincing. There is an obvious anti-consumer message in the film, the picture festooned with Christmas imagery which Kubrick makes tacky and overbearing. The first line in the film by Cruise is telling. "Honey, have you seen my wallet?" Bill spends a preposterous amount of money in the film (his wallet is like the TARDIS) but we see that he is a small fry when he is confronted with real wealth and the secret underworld of New York.

Early on he meets an old friend at the lavish Christmas party named Nick Nightingale (Todd Field) who dropped out of medical school while he was there and now plays piano at posh parties like this for the rich. "Yes, or in my case, never a doctor, never a doctor..." It's an awkward meeting because the two men are no longer equals in terms of status or money. The message is of course that it shouldn't really matter. The money drenched shadows behind the secret parties have all the money in the world but they have to wear masks at their orgies. There is no communication or intimacy. It's all aloof and distasteful. There are some things money can't buy.

Eyes Wide Shut feels more glossy and mainstream than some of Kubrick's other work despite the darkness. There is much going on and Kubrickians could spend years poring over the film looking for different meanings but it is the one film in his back catalogue that hasn't attained some sort of cult status.

THE EXORCISM (1972)

Dead of Night was a BBC anthology horror series of six episodes in the early seventies but - sadly - only three of these survive today. It's a great shame because if The Excorcism is anything to go by this was a high quality series with a terrific sense of atmosphere.

The Exorcism has two well to do couples staying at an old rural cottage to have Christmas dinner. But Christmas dinner is going to be ruined this year. There is a possession and the spirits seem to want to make a particular point about social justice and the rich exploiting the poor.

This drama is spare in terms of sets and camerawork but is rich in mood and director Don Taylor gets - in particular - a superb performance from Anna Cropper when she is taken over by the presence of ghostly spirits. This is a very talky drama but rewarding.

The wine might be blood, the turkey makes everyone ill, the power is cut, and strange things are never far away. The final ten minutes are remarkably haunting and present a satisfying conclusion that lingers in the memory. The Exorcism is a classic spooky BBC drama from the horror crazed seventies.

FANNY AND ALEXANDER (1982)

Fanny and Alexander is a drama by the legendary Swedish director Ingmar Bergman. There are two versions of this film - one a five hour miniseries and the other a three hour theatrical cut. You should definitely watch the longer version if you can. Bergman had a reputation for being gloomy but many of his films are magical and entrancing too. He directed classics like Wild Strawberries, Summer with Monika, and The Seventh seal.

The title Fanny and Alexander refers to a brother and sister growing up in Sweden in the early years of the 20th century. When their father dies their mother remarries but this man of the cloth turns out to be abusive towards Alexander. The film is somewhat autobiographical and so was a personal story to Bergman. Now, you might think that a five hour Swedish film with this synopsis AND directed by Bergman doesn't exactly sound like your idea of a good time but the film has some truly magical scenes and a section of the story takes place on Christmas Eve.

There's a huge canvas here with the family fully realised with their complex relationships. The story is often presented through the eyes of the children and children have considerably better imaginations than adults because they have yet to be diluted by too much harsh reality. As such, the film is often surreal, strange, but always entrancing.

Visually, this film is an absolute masterpiece with the set designs and costumes all perfect. In a way this film is almost an anthology, dealing as it does with different parts of the family. There are many themes in the film from religion, to death, to imagination, magic, and so on. Bergman is often associated with black and white films but this picture is colourful and vibrant. This is probably not going to be everyone's cup of tea but if you like films which tell a story through vignettes and different aspects of a family then you should find this a very rewarding experience.

FATHER CHRISTMAS (1991)

Father Christmas is a television animated film based on the books Father Christmas and Father Christmas Goes on Holiday by Raymond Briggs. I absolutely love this film and always watch it every Christmas. Father Christmas here is perfectly voiced by the late actor and comedian Mel Smith. In this film Father Christmas is not some vaguely supernatural character (though his reindeer can still fly of course!) living in the North Pole with thousands of elves but just an ordinary old man who lives in an ordinary semi-detached house somewhere in a street in Britain. He's a very British and human Father Christmas and is grumpily awoken by his alarm clock on Christmas Eve for what is his most important and arduous day of the year.

He lives with his cat and dog and has a couple of reindeer but that's about it as far as help goes. With his presents for everyone waiting out in the shed he must have his breakfast and prepare to later venture out into the cold and snow to make sure all of us - including the residents of Buckingham Palace - have a nice Christmas Day and get what we want. This being a very down to earth and human Father Christmas he grumbles a lot as he goes about his duties ('blooming chimneys!') but we know that deep down he loves his job and there is nothing else he'd rather be doing on this most special of nights.

I like the idea of making Father Christmas a normal person and it's fun to see him pottering about in his ordinary house having his breakfast and feeding his beloved pets (who the film manages to give real personality in Briggs' understated yet stylish way). The film is wonderful too when Santa has to go out into the night and deliver all of the presents and conjures up some great animation of his sleigh floating over snow dusted houses in the moonlight and Father Christmas battling with television aerials as he tries to climb inside chimneys!

The scenes where Father Christmas goes on holiday (to France, the United States, and Scotland) are great fun and there's an arrestingly surreal sequence where he has bizarre nightmares after over indulging in French cuisine. I think the scenes in Santa's house are especially nice and cosy here, especially when he has his own Christmas dinner ('Lovely grub!'), lights his pudding and basks in the warm glow of the fire in his favourite chair. It's always amusing and engaging to be in the company of our bearded hero - a very human Santa who listens to the radio as he peels his spuds and veg, grumbles about how parky it is outside and wistfully thinks of the summer and going on holiday as the snow and ice piles up outside. Father Christmas is a charming and cosy television classic.

FIVE CHARACTERS IN SEARCH OF AN EXIT (1961)

"Clown, hobo, ballet dancer, bagpiper, and an army major - a collection of question marks. Five improbable entities stuck together into a pit of darkness. No logic, no reason, no explanation; just a prolonged nightmare in which fear, loneliness and the unexplainable walk hand in hand through the shadows. In a moment we'll start collecting clues as to the whys, the whats and the wheres. We will not end the nightmare, we'll only explain it - because this is the Twilight Zone."

This is an episode of The Twilight Zone set at Christmas. It was written by Rod Serling and directed by Lamont Johnson. Five strangers - Army Major (William Windom), Clown (Murray Matheson), Ballerina (Susan Harrison), Tramp (Kelton Garwood), and Bagpiper (Clark Allen) - find themselves trapped together in a metal cylinder with no memory of how they got there. How did they end up in here? Where are they? And more to the point, how do they escape?

This episode's title is a variation on the Pirandello play Six Characters in Search of an Author. Five Characters in Search of an Exit is an enjoyably offbeat and surreal Twilight Zone with a memorably bizarre get out of jail ending. The strangeness of the situation the characters find themselves in here is always interesting and the preposterous costumes merely add to the off-kilter auara. The always solid William Windom is well cast as the nominal lead (his army officer is the most determined to escape) and Murray Matheson adds to the claustrophobia with his nutty clown character.

Five Characters in Search of an Exit might ultimately be an exercise in frustration but it isn't an episode you'll forget in a hurry. The spartan setting is in many ways the greatest strength of this episode in that the mystery is so perplexing and weird that you are immediately fascinated and curious to see what the explanation for this strange state of affairs is. The episode is at its most gripping when the characters (led by the army officer) make a determined attempt to escape. The twist at the end is so far out you can't help but just go along with it. Five Characters in Search of an Exit is a terrific little episode and up there with the most memorable Twilight Zone stories.

FROSTY THE SNOWMAN (1969)

This a television cartoon by Rankin/Bass which runs to about 25 minutes. It's quite a simple cartoon in terms of animation but has plenty of charm and has become a Christmas favourite. Most people will remember this because of the unmistakable voice of Jimmy Durante as the narrator.

The plot has a group of children, with the help of a magician and his rabbit, making a snowman come to life outside their school. The snowman is named Frosty but Frosty must somehow get to the North Pole otherwise he will melt. That's basically the plot of the cartoon and it's all agreeable enough. Santa makes an appearance before the end and there are some nice songs.

Kids will definitely enjoy this cartoon and because it doesn't go on for too long there's no danger of them getting bored. In fact, I think they'll probably be so lulled into the seasonal atmosphere and mission to get Frost to the North Pole that they won't even notice how long - or indeed how short - Frosty the Snowman actually is! They'll be far too busy just having a good time. The animation here is nothing elaborate but it does the job and has plenty of character and charm. Frosty the Snowman is just very likeable seasonal fare for younger viewers.

A GHOST STORY FOR CHRISTMAS (1971-1978)

A Ghost Story for Christmas is a strand of annual British short television films originally broadcast on BBC One between 1971 and 1978. The bulk of the stories were based on the work of M.R James but there was also a Dickens adaptation and two original screenplays. These films are perfect viewing for Christmas and usually run to about 45 minutes. This series began with The Stalls of Barchester. Dr Black (Clive Swift) is asked to catalogue Barchester Cathedral Library - well, look for things of notable interest anyway. It's a dull task until he stumbles across the diaries of Archdeacon Haynes.

The Stalls of Barchester doesn't enjoy the fame of the other BBC ghost stories for Christmas but it's very atmospheric and has a couple of good scares. The sinister sound effects and noises in this are especially nerve jangling. It's nicely directed with a brooding atmosphere and Robert Hardy is well cast as Haynes. The familiar pattern of secrets from the past infecting the present is solid enough but perhaps, ultimately, this isn't the most cherished and potent of the James stories. It's a fine spooky television adaptation though and not a bad place to start if this series of dramas is new to you. Some of the other ghost stories for Christmas are more immediate and memorable but this is still very worthwhile for those who enjoy slow burn horror and vintage television chillers.

A Warning to the Curious is probably the scariest of these episodes. This was again directed by Lawrence Gordon Clark. A treasure hunter digs up an old crown in Norfolk and unwittingly releases a sinister ghost that proves rather troublesome. There is a real aura of dread in this adaptation and once again this series of dramas proves that you don't need elaborate special effects or a lot of money to scare people. The phantom is more or less just a black clad figure with a hat but they manage to make him rather unsettling. The drama uses the landscapes of the area to great effect and Peter Vaughn is well cast as the archaeologist. Look out for Clive Swift too, returning to 'ghost stories' as Dr Black again.

Lost Hearts is one of the less effective of these episodes if still watchable. I enjoyed The Treasure of Abbot Thomas more though - this story having an amazing sense of atmosphere. The Ash Tree is also very solid and then we get a classic with The Signalman. This was directed by Lawrence Gordon Clark and regarded to be a spine tingling classic. Denholm Elliott is a signalman at a lonely railway station who is haunted by a figure who seems to anticipate accidents.

The Signalman is a superior drama beautifully directed with fantastic use of strange sound effects that amp up the already ghostly atmosphere. Bell vibrations are rather eerie. Denholm Elliott is excellent as the signalman and his isolation and sense of regret is vividly captured. There are some very striking images in the drama and The Signalman successfully captures a supernatural atmosphere of unease. This would make perfect late night viewing for Christmas or Halloween.

1977's Stigma is not quite a classic but it is very good. As ever, Lawrence Gordon Clark was in the director's chair. This is a rather atypical entry in the series as it is set in the present day. It is possibly the bleakest of the dramas and certainly the bloodiest. The story concerns a family moving to a country cottage where some ancient obelisks dot the nearby field. In the garden of their new home Katherine (Kate Binchy) insists that the workmen try to remove a huge menhir.

Well, as you may have guessed already, messing about with ancient mystical stones in the English countryside can never end very well in horror stories. When the stone is partially moved, Katherine feels a tremendous gust of wind and seems to go into a trance. Later on, she begins to seep blood despite no evidence of a wound.

Stigma is very low-key and bleak, which certainly generates a foreboding atmosphere, but the brevity of the drama is a slight problem as we never really get enough time to know these characters in order to care about them. One nice element though is the family have a teenage daughter but the daughter is left alone by the supernatural curse/stigmata. It would have been very predictable to have the daughter targeted by the supernatural.

Kate Binchy is quite good as Katherine and has an especially unsettling scene where she is in the bathroom trying to find the source of the blood she keeps losing. Peter Bowles plays the husband but he only has a few scenes. One would not place Stigma at the Ghost Stories for Christmas top table but the minimalist nature of the drama and cold aura it projects is certainly compelling. The last episode in this series was The Ice House. This had a new director and was an original story. It isn't as good as some of the others but it's worth a look. I would certainly recommended you watch all the episodes of A Ghost Story for Christmas. This series is rightly regarded to be a classic.

GREMLINS (1984)

Gremlins is a beloved 1984 horror/comedy film directed by Joe Dante and written by Chris Columbus. It was produced by Steven Spielberg. An inventor named Randall "Rand" Peltzer (Hoyt Axton) wants to buy a unique Christmas gift for his son Billy (Zach Galligan) and browses in an old store in Chinatown where he stumbles across a cute little creature known as a mowgai (in Cantonese Chinese, mogwai means devil, demon or gremlin). The old man who runs the store tells him it is not for sale but the man's grandson later makes a deal to sell it to Randall. He gives Randall a warning though concerning the creature. There are three things one must never do with a mogwai. It must never be exposed to bright light or water and must never be fed after midnight.

Well, as you may imagine, these rules eventually get broken and 'Gizmo', as the mowgai is named, hatches out dozens of other furry mogwai. However these creatures turn out to be not nearly as gentle as Gizmo and the small town of Kingston Falls is soon besieged by mischievous 'gremlins'...

Gremlins begins as a wonderful Capra-esque parody of small town life and then turns enjoyably dark when the gremlin mayhem kicks into gear. The original concept for Gremlins was apparently even more horrific. In early treatments the gremlins eat Billy's dog and decapitate his mother! I gather it was the producer Steven Spielberg who toned down some of the more gruesome elements. The set for the town in Gremlins was also used for Hill Valley in Back to the Future. It makes a nice playground for the gremlins to run amok in. Perhaps the most famous scene in the film comes when Billy's mother fights off the gremlins in her kitchen with the use of whatever appliances and tools are to hand. This sequence feels like a taste of what the original screenplay must have been like.

Each gremlin on the screen is an animatronic puppet that cost between $50,000 and $65,000 apiece. This film was consequently a nightmare production but in this CGI age the gremlins look fantastic and the old school special effects are very charming. Early tests included the idea of using monkeys in gremlin costumes. The monkeys were too obstreperous though so this was scrapped. One of the great things about Gremlins is the dark humour that filters through the action.

The 'stairlift' scene is a wonderful example. Phoebe Cates' (who plays Billy's co-worker and crush Kate) famous speech in the film about why she hates Christmas was not liked by either the studio or Steven Spielberg but Joe Dante fought his corner and kept it in the film. Steven Spielberg actually had to fight the studio to get Phoebe Cates in the film. The studio were reluctant to cast Cates because she was best known at the time for raunchy teen comedies.

Originally Stripe (the chief gremlin troublemaker) and Gizmo were to become the same character. It was changed so that there was a sympathetic gremlin. Zach Galligan and Phoebe Cates are very likeable as the leads and Hoyt Axton is great as Billy's inventor father. Look out for Dante regular Dick Miller as Murray Futterman. Corey Feldman also features in the film as Billy's friend Pete. Michael Winslow, the sound effects officer in Police Academy, provided some of the gremlin voices. They have great personality and feature in some memorable set pieces - like their rowdy bar antics and watching Snow White in a cinema populated entirely by gremlins.

I would like to mention the wonderful dog Barney also. Watch out for that dog in Gremlins. It has impeccable comic timing. Gremlins is a lot of fun with a great Christmas atmosphere and the deft mix of horror, satire, and humour. It's like a Steven Spielberg film given a slightly skewed makeover and Joe Dante (who had impressed Spielberg with The Howling) proves to be a great choice to direct.

THE GUARDIANS OF THE GALAXY CHRISTMAS SPECIAL (2022)

This is a special festive spin-off featuring the Marvel characters. It was directed by James Gunn. The Guardian of the Galaxy are a dysfunctional band of outlaws who take the Marvel universe in a more comedic sort of direction. Anyway, this 40 minute Christmas special has Mantis and Drax deciding to give Peter Quill a perfect Christmas gift by presenting him with his hero Kevin Bacon. Kevin Bacon is naturally none too thrilled about this though.

The Guardians of the Galaxy Holiday Special is a very slight affair and padded out with a number of songs by the Old 97's.

The stuff featuring Drax and Mantis kidnapping Kevin Bacon outstays its welcome in the end although it is fun when these two characters visit a bar. There also isn't enough of Rocket Racoon and groot in the special.

These quibbles aside though there is a terrific Christmas atmosphere throughout and the special is framed by some nice cartoon sequences. While this special struggles to justify its own existence at times it is a fun bonus for fans of these characters and you'd have to have a heart of stone not to enjoy the scenes where a Christmas lights display is arranged for Peter Quill.

HARRY POTTER AND THE GOBLET OF FIRE (2005)

Expecto patronum! This is a rather obvious inclusion as I suspect nearly everyone has seen the Harry Potter films by now. Harry Potter is now a $25 billion franchise but it had surprisingly humble origins. JK Rowling received several rejections from publishers before Harry Potter went into print. These publishers (who must still be kicking themselves) thought that Harry Potter and the Philosopher's Stone was a trifle on the long side for a children's book. They also, clearly, failed to anticipate the huge global appeal of Harry Potter. Remarkably, the initial Hardback run by Bloomsbury of the first Harry Potter book published only 500 copies. Its eventual success though was nothing short of astonishing.

Goblet of Fire was directed by Mike Newell and has a number of Christmas themed sequences. The Potter movie franchise made an uncertain start but managed to really find its feet after Chris Columbus departed as the director and new filmmakers were brought in. The studio wanted The Goblet of Fire to be made into two separate films but the director Mike Newell insisted he could convey the story in one film. Goblet of

Fire was the largest grossing movie of 2005 and got pretty good reviews. It's certainly a nice film to watch at Christmas. Mike Newell said he was inspired by Bollywood films on Goblet on Fire. He wanted to make it the most colourful of the Potter movies.

Ralph Fiennes says he nearly turned down the part of Voldemort because he didn't know anything about Harry Potter! In French, Voldemort means "Flight of Death". In this film version of Goblet of Fire, Hermione wears a pink dress to the Yule Ball rather than a blue one (as in the book). This was because the costume designer thought that blue didn't suit Emma Watson and the set background was also blue so it would have been difficult for the dress to be noticed. Some fans felt that Hermione's Cinderella moment at the ball in Goblet of Fire didn't really work in the films because Hermione is quite plain in the books whereas Emma Watson looks more like a catalogue model!

In the Yule Ball scenes in Goblet of Fire, we only see Harry Potter from the waist up. This is because Daniel Radcliffe didn't have time for dance lessons and so didn't know the footwork and moves for this sequence. The rock band at the Yule-Ball In Goblet of Fire is made up of real musicians from Pulp and Radiohead. Goblet of Fire has a nice mix of locations, great special effects, and the usual stellar supporting cast of British thespians. It's certainly one of the best of the Potter films.

HOME ALONE (1990)

Well, I suppose Home Alone HAS to go in this book somewhere or other. It is far from my favourite Christmas film but it does have that cosy feelgood seasonal aura one expects of a family movie from the John Hughes stable. Hughes wrote the film and it was directed by Chris Columbus (who would go to direct an even bigger family movie when he got the gig to bring Harry Potter to the big screen).

Does anyone not know the plot of this film by now? A kid named Kevin McCallister (Macaulay Culkin) is unwittingly left all alone in his house when his family go on a Christmas vacation to Paris but leave him behind by accident. The house is targeted by a couple of burglars (played by Joe Pesci and Daniel stern respectively) but they find they've bitten off more than they can chew with the resourceful Kevin.

There's a great cast here (look out for a cameo by John Candy) and Macaulay Culkin was certainly a talented and charismatic child actor. Home alone is an old-fashioned slapstick sort of comedy at times and although there probably isn't enough here to make it a film that adults would return to much it is a film that kids should enjoy a lot. The film looks terrific too.

It does have that very John Hughes trope where everyone seems to be rich and live in a giant house (and how many of us could actually afford to go on holiday to Paris over Christmas with our ENTIRE family?!) but it would be a trifle churlish to nitpick this film too much because it merely wants to be a pleasant seasonal family film with some laughs. In those aims it succeeds admirably. The movie was actually a huge financial hit at the time and spawned a franchise - with mixed results. A sequel - Home Alone 2: Lost in New York - was rushed into production but got poor reviews despite doing well at the box-office. After a (largely forgotten) third film with an all new cast, Home Alone eventually became one of those straight to video/DVD sort of franchises.

HOME FOR THE HOLIDAYS (1972)

Home for the Holidays was directed by John Llewellyn Moxey and written by Joseph Stefano. A dying old man named

Benjamin Morgan (Walter Brennan) summons his daughters to his mansion at Christmas because he believes his wife Elizabeth (Julie Harris) is trying to kill him. The sisters are Alex (Eleanor Parker), Frederica (Jessica Walter), Joanna (Jill Haworth) and Christine (Sally Field). The sisters settle into the home and try to gauge if Elizabeth really is secretly plotting the demise of their father. It is the sisters though who start to be killed off one by one...

This is a fun TV film that actually seems to anticipate the slasher trend of the seventies and early eighties. It is diluted through the prism of television of course but you do get someone killed by a pitchfork, drowning by bathtub, and Sally Field being chased through the countryside by a murderous maniac on a dark stormy night. There's a terrific performance by Julie Harris too as the under suspicion Elizabeth. Harris gives her performance just the right amount of ambiguity. The old horror staple of a dark and stormy night in an old big house is all wheeled out here to good effect.

The film shrewdly doesn't take too long to start killing the sisters off and amping up the intrigue. It manages to avoid being too talky and static by cutting straight to the chase as best it can. The actresses playing the sisters are all competent in their roles although Eleanor Parker seems too old to be a sibling to the others. A baby faced Sally Field could pass as her grandaughter. You'll notice too that Jill Haworth's American accent keeps slipping. Sometimes she sounds English and other times American. There are a few ripe melodramatic acting moments but it all seems part of the charm. You get the impression that the actors here are having a good time.

If I had to pinpoint a weakness in Home for the Holidays it would be that I worked out quite early on who I thought was responsible for the murders and this assumption turned out to be true. I don't think one needs to be Columbo to have a good idea of what is really happening in the house but it's by no means a fault in any of the performances and doesn't really negate the fun of the film too much. Despite the constrictive location (basically the house and its immediate surroundings) the film is well directed and inventive in taking us to different parts of the house and the chase scene with Sally Field is well staged and quite tense.

If you love the old made for television thriller and horror films produced in the United States in the seventies then you should get around to Home for the Holidays if you haven't already done so. The film is a lot of fun and interesting in the way that it seems to signpost a horror trend that was lurking just around the corner.

HOW THE GRINCH STOLE CHRISTMAS! (1966)

How the Grinch Stole Christmas! is an animated film based on the book of the same name by Dr Seuss. This television cartoon was produced and directed by Chuck Jones and has become a beloved Christmas staple. It runs to about 25 minutes. The story has the Grinch (who sort of looks like a green goblin cat) becoming so irritated by the residents of Whoville enjoying Christmas that he decides he will put a stop to the festivities once and for all by sealing all their gifts and decorations and dumping them atop the mountain where he lives in a cave. The Grinch will come to learn though tat the spirit of Christmas is a lot more durable and profound than he'd been led to believe.

The animation in this cartoon is not elaborate by modern standards but it has bags of personality and plenty of Christmas atmosphere. The story has a nice warm twist at the end and the fairly modest running time means that the cartoon never threatens to outstay its welcome. Children will certainly enjoy this cartoon and adults should get a kick out of it too. The absolute icing on the cake here is the presence of the great Boris Karloff as the narrator and the voice of the

Grinch. How the Grinch Stole Christmas! is a classic
Christmas cartoon and perfect viewing for the festive season.

IN BRUGES (2008)

In Bruges is a 2008 black comedy directed and written by
Martin McDonagh. The film revolves around two professional
hitmen named Ray (Colin Farrell) and Ken (Brendan Gleeson).
Ken is older than Ray and something of a mentor to him. Ray
bungled a previous hit when he accidentally shot a boy in a
church and so, along with Ken, has been sent to the Belgian
city of Bruges to lay low and await instructions from their boss
Harry (Ralph Fiennes).

Ray is bewildered by the fact that they are in Bruges of all
places but Ray seems to enjoy the old charm charm of the
town. It is clearly Christmas as Bruges is bedecked in lights
and decorations. The two men question their life choices and
chances of redemption but the real drama is about to begin...

To say too much about In Bruges would be to give the plot
away but this is an interesting and very absorbing film which
defies any strict definition. It's a comedy, a drama, a thriller,
and more besides. The film is often very funny and Farrell and
Gleeson have amazing chemistry together as these very
different hitmen. They have some bizarre little adventures in
Bruges and both wrest with the reality of what they do for a
living.

It is clearly not easy to be a killer and somehow the Christmas
backdrop makes the knowledge of this all the more difficult to
live with. The film's only dubious note is Ralph Fiennes as
their somewhat unhinged boss Harry. Fiennes is somewhat
over the top in this part and clearly seems to be trying to
channel Ben Kingsley as Don Logan in the crime film Sexy
Beast. That aside though, In Bruges is a lot of fun and one of
the more unusual Christmas themed films you are likely to

encounter.

IRON MAN 3 (2013)

Iron Man 3 (or "Iron Man Three" as the end credits would
have it) is the third go around for Robert Downey Jr's
irreverent take on the cult Marvel Comics superhero. The
major change for this one is that Jon Favreau has been
replaced in the director's chair by Shane (The Last Boy Scout)
Black and the witty Black (who also co-wrote the screenplay)
brings a much more flippant and insouciant air to
proceedings, the humour quotient amped. I strongly suspect
this is the only Hollywood blockbuster you'll ever watch that
has a joke about Croydon. Black is more interested in
character interaction, dialogue and giving people funny things
to say than Iron Man shenanigans and this is both a strength
and a weakness. It's a colourful and amusing entry in the
superhero stakes and zips past in entertaining fashion but
ultimately it does feel more like a Shane Black film than an
Iron Man film. As with all Shane Black films too this movie is
set at Christmas.

While general audiences will have a lot of fun I think the pesky
fanboys will be less forgiving of the gaping plot holes, the
treatment of certain characters and the willing disregard Black
displays for the Marvel film universe that has been unfurled
over the last several years. I found myself quite torn in that I
enjoyed the film a lot while it was playing but did find myself
nitpicking when I thought about it afterwards. Although Iron
Man 3 is supposed to be the start of Phase 2 for Marvel it feels
much more like the last gasp of Phase 1. The film is set a few
months after the events of The Avengers and finds multi-
billionaire industrialist and inventor extraordinaire Tony Stark
suffering from sleepless nights and anxiety attacks whenever
he remembers the New York battle with that alien armada and
having to fly through the worm hole to save the world.

This extended encounter with Gods, monsters and aliens has left him feeling vulnerable and worried about the threats he might have to face in the future. Can he keep those close to him safe? He is after all just an ordinary man behind the high-tech armour, jet boots and repulsor rays. Tony has been spending the sleepless nights endlessly creating and tinkering with his Iron Man armours and is now up to Mark 42 - a prototype suit that can be remote controlled by Stark's thoughts in encephalo fashion and can also quickly attach itself to him in flying pieces during an emergency situation.

Trouble is soon looming for our preoccupied insomniac hero though in the form of two villains. The Mandarin (Ben Kingsley) is a shadowy Osma Bin Laden like terrorist who has been striking deep in the heart of America while Aldrich Killian (Guy Pearce) is a rival businessman who has been dabbling in a dangerous and powerful genetics altering technology called Extremis. When Stark's lavish beachside home is attacked by helicopters and his Iron Man armours are apparently destroyed, Tony finds himself all alone with only the battered and damaged - not to mention untested - Mark 42. Can our bearded wisecracking hero still save the day?

What's good about Iron Man 3? Well, Robert Downey Jr is always funny and charismatic and could probably play this role in his sleep by now. I like the way the film is constructed with Stark narrating the story to an offscreen listener (stay for the post credit Easter egg to see who) and the "Classic Bond" fan in me loved the old school James Bond riffs that Black seems to draw on.

There is a spectacular mid-air plane sequence involving Iron Man that scores points for using real skydivers rather than CGI and the interplay of the supporting actors with Downey Jr is relaxed and witty. Gwyneth Paltrow is starting to come into her own as Pepper Potts and it's good to see Jon Favreau in front of the camera again as Happy Hogan. Don Cheadle is not the most convincing action lead but he makes Rhodes feel more like a friend of Stark than the dull Terrance Howard did in the previous films and he also gets to don the War Machine armour (here made to look like Iron Patriot from the comics).

Guy Pearce enjoyably hams it up as Killian and I liked the wonderfully laid-back turn by James Badge Dale as Killian's main henchman Savin. You are never too far away from a decent laugh either. My favourite Shane Black line in the film? When one of the villain's henchmen says - "Don't shoot! Seriously, I don't even like working here. They are so weird!" I think the biggest problem for fans of the comics is going to be the depiction of The Mandarin and in this regard Iron Man 3 does feel rather like an elaborate joke aimed purely at annoying fanboys.

In the comics, The Mandarin is Iron Man's deadliest and most famous enemy. He is to Tony Stark what Moriarty is to Sherlock Holmes or Blofeld is to James Bond. The Mandarin is a Chinese wizard with flowing robes who looks like Fu Manchu or Lo Pan and has ten magical rings that give him access to alien technology. Now, someone at Marvel has obviously decided that The Mandarin is too much of a racial stereotype to get away with these days and for understandable economic reasons China is the last place modern Hollywood wants to offend. So The Mandarin here has been refashioned as a more racially ambiguous villain who seems to operate from the Middle East. Disappointing to think we'll never see The Mandarin from the comics onscreen but all well and good I suppose.

Ben Kingsley's line reading as The Mandarin is rather intriguing too and it appears as if a very memorable villain is still going to emerge despite the changes. However, I suspect that the ultimate arc of The Mandarin here is going to split audiences down the middle. General viewers will like it and fans of the comics will not. It's just a shame though that the full potential of The Mandarin will probably never appear in one of these Marvel films now. I have to be pedantic for a moment and run through a few other quibbles that bugged me. Why are Tony's armours so fragile in this film? We've seen his

Iron Man suits battle alien technology and even stand up to a scuffle with The Mighty Thor in The Avengers. Here they seem to fall apart at the drop of a hat. It seems inconsistent with the previous films.

Also, having established that the world is full of superheroes and that there is a government agency to keep an eye on superpowered or alien threats, where is SHIELD is this film? It seems a trifle odd and convenient that they just vanish while Tony Stark is battling the Extremis villains - especially as Air Force One is hijacked in the film. And Tony Stark spends precious little time as Iron Man and for most of the film runs around like a government spy trying to get the drop on Killian. I suspect that the thesp in Robert Downey Jr wanted as few scenes as possible with Iron Man capers and prefers to have his face onscreen.

Another quibble is that when they have a sequence where Iron Man does something and then we learn that Tony was merely remote controlling the suit from a cupboard (or something) it's simply not as dramatically satisfying as having him actually in the suit doing these things. I could point out too that the Guy Pearce villain is an exact carbon copy of The Riddler from Batman Forever. It is extraordinary how they pilfer the whole Riddler arc lock stock and barrel, even down to Killian as an uber nerd meeting Stark early on and becoming bent on revenge from a perceived snub. Still, Pearce is a lot of fun and chews up the scenery in every scene he's in. The film doesn't make much sense in the end as two of the major developments in the last act are - when you think about it - things that Tony could presumably have done at any time he wanted to. So, essentially, he didn't even need to get so battered and bruised and into so much trouble and could have wrapped this all up much earlier.

The big action set-piece at the end is somewhat of a mess but - like Iron Man 3 in general - it's fun and you forgive Black some of his excesses and inability to grasp logic and coherence because he constantly throws you funny lines and keeps the film full of energy. I enjoyed the thoroughly unsentimental depiction of the President (played as a bit of a sleaze by William Sadler) and Rebecca Hall adds some class to the film as a scientist who we are introduced to early on in a flashback set in Switzerland. Tony Stark does get a kid sidekick for part of the film but mercifully this doesn't play out nearly as bad as it sounds. Overall, there are far too many plot holes for this to be considered anywhere near a classic but the film always coasts along in enjoyable and entertaining fashion, never quite as sassy as it thinks it is but certainly invested with a lot more wit than your average popcorn blockbuster fare.

IT'S A WONDERFUL LIFE (1947)

It's a Wonderful Life is perhaps the ultimate Christmas film. It was directed by Frank Capra and tells the story of George Bailey (James Stewart). George lives in the small town of Bedford falls and is a pillar of the community. However, when he has some bad luck and runs into financial trouble he contemplates suicide and wishes that he'd never been born. His problems attract the attention of a guardian angel (Henry Travers). George will see exactly what would have transpired in Bedford Falls if he hadn't been born. The place would have been an awful lot worse without his good deeds.

It's a Wonderful Life has a beautifully cosy and warm Christmas atmosphere but it's an interesting film in that it deals with dark themes (depression, suicide, hopelessness, money troubles) but still manages to be thoroughly uplifting and life affirming. George has been a hero to those around him but he can't seem to see that for himself.

One of the nice things about this film is that it shows us how the real heroes in life are just ordinary people who go out of their way to be kind and help people. George is one such person. You can't imagine anyone other than James Stewart playing George and he gives one of his most memorable performances in this classic movie. The message of it's a Wonderful Life is that every person is important and just occasionally they all need to be reminded of that.

KLAUS (2019)

Klaus is a 2019 Spanish-American animated Christmas film written and directed by Sergio Pablos. The film takes place in 19th century and concerns the bunglingtrainee postman Jesper Johansen. Jesper is sent to the remote town of Smeerensburg and is tasked with delivering a huge amount of letters - otherwise he will be cut off from the family fortune.

The folks in Smeerensburg are a miserable bunch who are always fighting and arguing. One day, Jesper stumbles across a reclusive man named Klaus who makes toys. Jesper delivers one of the toys made by Klaus to a local child and soon the other children in the town start writing letters to the toymaker in the hope that they will get a gift too. Jesper and Klaus must team up to make sure these children get their toys and so the legend of Father Christmas is born. Can they make the mean spirited people of Smeerensburg change their ways?

Klaus deservedly drew rave review and won multiple awards when it was released in 2019. Most of us probably feel like we have had to sit through a few too many Christmas animated films in our time but this one is quite unlike anything you ever seen before. Klaus is remarkably stylish with amazing use of shadows and texture. Every frame of this film is a work of art which is a delight for the viewer to take in and enjoy.

The characters have real personality and there some decent laughs along the way. Most of all though Klaus works because it is a clever and inventive 'origin' film which takes an enjoyable look at how the legend of Santa Claus might have begun. Although this film is still relatively new it seems destined to take its place as a Christmas classic for decades to come.

KNOWING ME, KNOWING YULE (1995)

Knowing Me, Knowing Yule is a special Christmas edition of the spoof BBC chat show featuring Steve Coogan's memorable comic creation Alan Partridge. Partridge is like a composite of every awful, bland, fame hungry television presenter who ever existed. Partridge is vain, shallow, tactless, talentless, irritable, and liable to put his foot in his mouth at any moment. He is basically the worst person in the world to host a chat show but that's the joke. Alan thinks he's a consummate professional born to do this!

Knowing Me, Knowing Yule is a lot of fun and finds Alan's attempts to do a classic festive special (the set is a Christmas mock-up of his living room complete with log fire!) predictably fall apart at the seams. Along the way Alan engages in some shameless product placement, has to put up with a drag queen chef who keeps dropping innuendos, and must also interview Tony Hayers - the new BBC Chief Commissioning Editor. Well, you just KNOW that Alan is going to mess that interview up and annoy Hayers!

Alan's attempts at having the world's largest Christmas cracker pulled and then sing The Twelve Days of Christmas also go disastrously wrong. If you enjoy the character of Alan Partridge then this is great fun. I still probably like the early Partridge radio chat shows the best but this early television chat show and the first season of I'm Alan Partridge are definitely the golden years of the Partridge character.

KRAMPUS (2015)

Krampus is a 2015 Christmas themed horror film directed by Michael Dougherty. Dougherty directed the brilliant Halloween themed anthology horror film Trick 'r Treat and although Krampus isn't as good as that earlier work it's still a pretty good effort and rich in Christmas atmosphere. Krampus is one of those 'mild' horror films too that can be watched by people of all ages.

In European folklore, Krampus is a half-goat, half-demon monster that punishes misbehaving children at Christmastime. In this film, the Enel family are preparing for Christmas but seem to evoke the wrath of the Krampus legend through their lack of Christmas spirit. This culminates in the son, young Max (Emjay Anthony), who is the only one who actually seems to like Christmas, becoming so dismayed by his relaives he declares that he hates Christmas too.

You know, I can actually empathise with Max. We've probably all had that experience where we try to have a magical time at Christmas but are brought down to earth by miserable people who treat Christmas like any other day and seem incapable of stepping out of harsh reality for a few days.

Anyway, Krampus is not what you would call a classic but it is a well made and likeable film with a fantastic wintry aura and some stylish Christmas horror flourishes. There's a solid cast here built around Adam Scott and Toni Collette as the parents and although the film is a bit slow to get going it is worth sticking with as it does get better as it goes on. One could argue that Dougherty should have considered making this an anthology film like Trick 'r Treat but then maybe he didn't want to make it seem like he was repeating himself.

Krampus is certainly one of the most Christmassy horror films you'll encounter and although it isn't the most original movie it does at least do something different from the usual

Christmas horror trope of turning Santa into a homocidal maniac. Krampus is pretty good fun once it gets going and is definitely worth a look.

THE LEGEND OF HELL HOUSE (1973)

The Legend of Hell House is a 1973 British horror film directed by John Hough and adapted by Richard Matheson from his own novel. The film is much in the vein of The Haunting and House on Haunted Hill and revolves around an investigation into a spooky, fog-shrouded country mansion. The investigation takes place at Christmas.

The plot has the wealthy but dying Rudolph Deutsch (Roland Culver) setting a challenge for physicist and parapsychology expert Dr Lionel Barrett (Clive Revill). Deutsch has a large bet (100,000 pounds) with Barrett and will pay out if the physicist can prove or disprove life after death. He asks Barrett to stay in an abandoned haunted mansion for a week to see if he can detect anything and the house he chooses is the most haunted house in the world - The Belasco House, better known as Hell House and "The Mount Everest of haunted houses."

Barrett is joined in Hell House by his wife Ann (Gayle Hunnicutt), medium Florence Tanner (Pamela Franklin), who is eager to make contact with any spirits in the mansion, and psychic medium Benjamin Fischer (Roddy McDowall), who was the only survivor of a previous investigation into the house twenty years before. "I was the only one to make it out of here alive and sane in 1953 and I will be the only one to make it out of here alive and sane this time," says the less than cheerful Fischer.

Imagine a slightly camper, colour, British version of The Haunting that isn't as good and you aren't far off describing

The Legend of Hell House which, while not a classic, is a solid entry in the haunted house stakes and a decent film in its own right. In its favour is a brooding atmosphere, some impressive sets and a spooky electronic score by Delia Derbyshire and Brian Hodgson.

The opening sequence of the characters arriving at Hell House and looking through the iron gates and mist towards spires and towers is nicely done and immediately sets up an eerie air of dread, continued when the group are greeted upon arrival by a creepy gramophone recording by a notorious previous owner of the house - the sadistic Emeric Belasco. "Welcome to my house. I'm delighted you could come. I'm certain you will find your stay here most illuminating. Think of me as your unseen servant, and believe that during your stay here I shall be with you in spirit. May you find the answer that you seek. It is here, I promise you."

Belasco vanished into thin air many years ago after infecting the house with evil through his obstreperous and unusual lifestyle choices. "Drug addiction, alcoholism, sadism, bestiality, mutilation, murder, vampirism, necrophilia, cannibalism, not to mention a gamut of sexual goodies. Shall I go on?" says Fischer when asked to supply a capsule biography of old Belasco. It appears, after a seance, that the spirit of Daniel Belasco, son of Emeric, roams the house and the younger Belasco soon begins to make life difficult for the temporary new occupants of Hell House, attempting to bump off Dr Barrett by various means and making all manner of strange things happen to Miss Tanner.

Revill's parapsychology expert Lionel Barrett is the dedicated and logical man of science although his neglect of his wife is soon picked up on by the house, the ghostly presence turning Anne into a rampant nymphomaniac who disrobes at the drop of a hat and keeps trying to seduce Roddy McDowall's geeky Fischer. Fischer is still traumatized by his last visit to Hell House and has erected a physic wall around himself for protection. He doesn't want to be there at first but slowly builds up an anger against the house and becomes more determined. McDowell is suitably aloof and eccentric throughout and his earnest (if slightly melodramatic) performance is a boost to the film.

Although the inanimate objects taking on a ghostly life of their own, creaky noises and swinging chandelier capers are all familiar from other films in the same (no pun intended) spirit, this is certainly very competently done with unusual camera angles and some tight editing, plus the enjoyably menacing electronic soundtrack. The Legend of Hell House is more of a psychological horror where we never actually see ghosts or monsters and what we imagine is always much scarier than what we see.

There is a Nigel Kneale quality to the film with the battle between science and the supernatural and this element is further deployed (and the film becomes slightly dafter and more vaguely sci-fi) when Barrett unveils a 'reverser' machine, a big box like something out of a Gerry Anderson television show, which he believes will drain the house of its psychic energy and send the spirit of Belasco's dead son, Daniel, away.

The house is a gigantic battery "full of mindless, directionless power" and Dr Barrett believes his machine will suck the energy out and set the house free from the evil that lurks there. It's enjoyable to see the controlled Barrett attempt to battle these dark forces - though with warnings from Fischer. "Belasco doesn't like it, his people don't like it, and they will fight back and they will kill you. So listen to me. You just leave that damn machine alone and you spend the rest of the week resting, doing nothing. When Sunday comes, you tell old Deutsch anything he wants to hear and bank the money. If you try anything else, you will be a dead man, with a dead wife at your side!"

Barrett believes that the mediums are conducting the electrical energy in the house and seems largely unconcerned with all the doom laden warnings. One nice touch in the film is having the two mediums, Fischer and Miss Tanner, disagree on the nature of the haunting and which course of action to take.

Flaws in The Legend of Hell House? Clive Revill is perhaps a tad wooden and unmemorable as Dr Barrett - a more urbane choice of actor might have worked better, like Peter Bowles for instance who turns up as Culver's snobby lawyer early in the film. Pamela Franklin is good though as Miss Tanner, who becomes like a magnet for the energy in the house and is also attacked by a possessed cat.

Michael Gough also makes a cameo near the end although the resolution of the film is not its biggest card and is fairly ludicrous when you actually think about it. The ending is really rather flawed - although not entirely devoid of fun. On the whole though, although a tad daft and derivative in places, I like The Legend of Hell House despite its evident flaws. A fun film to watch late at night.

THE LEMON DROP KID (1951)

The Lemon Drop Kid is a 1951 American comedy film based on the short story of the same name by Damon Runyon. The film was directed by Sidney Lanfield - although it seems to be an open secret that Frank Tashlin finished the picture. This is a Bob Hope comedy is which he plays a conman and hustler known as the Lemon Drop Kid (he got this name because he always has lemon drops in his pocket).

Our comic hero ends up on the wrong side of a gangster in the run up to Christmas and must somehow raise a large sum of money. To this end he comes up with a charity scam involving dressing up as Santa Claus. The plot doesn't really matter here too much. This is just light breezy fun with Hope in good form in his usual fast talking, quip dispensing, slightly cowardly screen persona. Hope was a great screen comic actor and probably only second to Groucho Marx at this sort of stuff.

This is not one of Hope's very best films but it is fun and amusing and there are plenty of Christmas themed capers with the Santa shenanigans. Hope sings Silver Bells, there are courtroom antics, Santas Claus impersonators aplenty, and generally amusing hijinks. If you are looking for some Christmas themed laughs then you could do a lot worse than give this pleasant and funny film a whirl.

LITTLE WOMEN (1994)

Little Women was directed by Gillian Armstrong and based on Louisa May Alcott's 1868-69 two-volume novel of the same title. There have been three versions of this story and all are worth watching but this is one I've always been the most familiar with. This a sentimental and enjoyable drama about the March sisters growing up after the Civil War. There is plenty of Christmas cheer in the film and a top notch cast with Winona Ryder, Susan Sarandon, Christian Bale, John Neville, Kirsten Dunst, and Claire Danes among others.

This is what you might describe as a classy tearjerker and sort of like a big-budget Hollywood version The Waltons. I'm probably doing the film an injustice with that description as Little Women is a terrific film with many memorable moments. Winona Ryder is great in the film and I love Clare Danes as Beth March too. Many fans of the book like this adaptation the best because it is very faithful to the source novel.

The cosy Christmas themed scenes in this film are on the icing on the cake and make Little Women a wonderful addition to any festive viewing plans. this is also an enjoyable film because it gives a raft of talented female actors a real spotlight. I would certainly recommend you watch the more recent remake of this too because that is very good too but the 1994 version of Little Women will always be the one closest to my heart.

THE LONG KISS GOODNIGHT (1996)

The Long Kiss Goodnight is an action thriller directed by Renny Harlin from a script by Shane Black. Geena Davis plays Samantha Caine, a schoolteacher in a small town. Samantha has a boyfriend and young daughter. Eight years previously she was washed up on the beach pregnant with no memory who who she really was. The puzzled and curious Samantha, despite the fact that her current life is pretty good, has hired a private detective named Mitch (Samuel L. Jackson) to try and find out who she actually is.

During the Christmas holiday, Samantha is involved in a car accident and suffers a concussion. When she wakes up she begins to realise that she is highly skilled in using a knife and seems to know all about guns. Her past is about to catch up with up with her because Samantha is really a CIA assassin who vanished eight years ago.

This film rather anticipates The Bourne Identity and even Kill Bill and is one of the more underrated action films of the 1990s. Geena Davis makes a great action heroine as a sort of female Jason Bourne (though with more personality than the tabula rasa Bourne) and there are some terrific action sequences and fights. Renny Harlin really loves blowing stuff up and you get plenty of that here.

A link between this movie and the Bourne films is that Samantha finds a bag containing her secret agent items and there's another link too in the form of Brian Cox as a government bigwig (Cox was in the Bourne films). Davis is fun when she dyes her hair to become the badass CIA operative Charlie and - best of all - there are plenty of Christmas trappings in the film with snow, sleighs, Christmas lights and so on. If you want a Christmas themed action movie to watch this holiday season and feel like you have watched Die Hard too many times then give The Long Kiss Goodnight a try instead.

LOVE'S GREAT ADVENTURE (2020)

Love's Great Adventure is an episode of the anthology show Inside No.9. Love's Great Adventure is what you might describe as a kitchen-sink drama. It is much more realistic and plausible than most episodes of Inside No.9. Steve Pemberton said that the films of Ken Loach were an influence and one can also see the influence of soap operas, 'stock' BBC & ITV 9pm British family themed dramas, and even perhaps a hint of The Royle Family. Love's Great Adventure tells a very human and down to earth story and eschews the comedy and horror we tend to associate with this show. Unusually for this show, Love's Great Adventure features (Patrick aside I suppose) characters who are warm and caring with no haunted pasts or dark deeds lurking in the cupboard.

The use of a Christmas advent calendar in the story evokes The 12 Days of Christine but it is possible that this is deliberate misdirection from Shearsmith & Pemberton as Love's Great Adventure is not fantastical or supernatural in the slightest. Shearsmith & Pemberton have said that the real twist in Love's Great Adventure is the fact that it doesn't have a twist or suddenly wrongfoot the audience with some outlandish reveal. There is definitely a reveal in Love's Great Adventure but, interestingly, this reveal is something that could plausibly happen and also something that happens offscreen. If we aren't paying attention we could almost miss this detail. Love's Great Adventure is essentially a deliberate attempt to do a different type of Inside No.9 episode and not give the audience what they might expect.

In this episode, Trevor (Pemberton) and Julia (Debbie Rush)

are trying to get ready for Christmas but money is tight and things are not easy. They are looking after their daughter Mia (Gabby French) and grandson Connor (Olly Hudson-Croker) but ever present in their thoughts is their absent son Patrick (Bobby Schofield) - who is Connor's father. Patrick (we presume) has had issues with drugs and now owes money to an especially nasty and dangerous loanshark...

Love's Great Adventure is the lowest rated episode of series five on IMDB - which I personally find quite baffling. One could argue that this is the best 'dramatic' episode of Inside No.9 ever made. It feels somewhat like Diddle Diddle Dumpling in tone and atmosphere but is warmer and less obtuse. Love's Great Adventure's contains one of the best performances Steve Pemberton has ever given on this show. He is completely believable as the working-class grandfather trying to get by and his scenes with Bobby Schofield as Patrick in particular are some of the most purely dramatic and powerful that Inside No.9 has ever produced.

We get little daily snippets of this family's life in the run up to Christmas and the cast make this family completely believe. Debbie Rush is terrific too - rarely do you see an onscreen couple that seem so authentic and real as Trevor and Julia. Even the child actor Olly Hudson-Croker is believable and impressive as little Connor. Love's Great Adventure is a reminder that shrewd casting (allied of course to strong writing) can go an awful long way sometimes. It's an impressive feat to make these characters seem so real and vivid in such a short amount of time.

Although some viewers were apparently disappointed by the lack of an overt twist, this is actually one of the great strengths of Love's Great Adventure. We keep expecting something truly bizarre to happen but it never quite does. When we realise at the end what Debbie may (or even may not) have done it feels perfectly satisfying as a way to conclude this story. Love's Great Adventure didn't need one of these characters to be revealed as a serial killer or a werewolf or something just for the sake of a big twist. To do so would have been to undercut the incredible verisimilitude of the drama we have been watching.

The 'twist' in Love's Great Adventure is very understated, almost throwaway and casual in its delivery. You could easily have missed this detail if you were not paying close attention. This reveal is simultaneously dark and uplifting. Something horrible happened but it was done out of love and maybe even had some twisted cosmic karma. One of the great strengths of this episode is that you genuinely have no idea where it is heading. The lives of these characters are offered to us in small parcels so that we have to fill in some of the blanks for ourselves. When Patrick does return home and reveals that a dangerous loanshark is after him there is a very tense scene where Trevor hears something at night and wonders if someone might be in the garden or trying to get into the house. What this episode does wonderfully well is tease moments and scenarios like this and then pull back on them. This keeps us on edge but prevents the drama from ever tilting over into anything too outlandish.

It was a brave move to attempt a very 'straight' episode of Inside No.9 like this but the writing and performances are well up to the task. Love's Great Adventure also offers a very realistic and balanced depiction of ordinary working-class life that is neither patronising nor full of clichés. These are just ordinary decent folk who live month to month and sometimes struggle with all the bills. That's basically life for the vast majority of us so we identify with these characters and see elements of our own family life in the various scenes set in the house.

There's a very touching scene in the episode where Julia can't afford a prom dress her daughter Mia wants and so makes one herself - something which takes a lot of time and effort. When the dress is revealed we see that Mia is disappointed it isn't the real dress she wanted but she tries to hide her dismay. Julia is embarrassed that she couldn't buy her daughter the real dress and knows that Mia will probably never wear the dress she made because she would feel foolish among her friends. There's such a wide range of emotions provoked by this simple and touching scene.

Reece Shearsmith take a back seat in this episode as uncle Alex - who gives Mia driving lessons. He will though play a pivotal part in the informing us of the resolution. Shearsmith has a nice moment where Alex refuses to accept his fee for Mia's driving lessons. This episode is not Shearsmith & Pemberton in comic mode but there are a few amusing moments where the family joke around together. The ups and downs of family life are wonderfully authentic in Love's Great Adventure. The family, like all families, sometimes argue and bicker but, ultimately, their bond to one another is stronger than any trouble that might come their way. Love's Great Adventure is a reminder of how versatile Inside No.9 is as a show. After the grotesque black comedy of Death Be Not Proud we get this restrained but highly rewarding kitchen-sink drama.

Love's Great Adventure clearly wasn't for everyone but it is without question one of the best acted and most realistic episodes of Inside No.9 in the show's history.

Sadly, this seemed to be the least favourite series five episode for a number of viewers but Love's Great Adventure is a great little drama and arguably one of the most underrated Inside No.9 entries in the history of the show. It's difficult to think of an episode where Steve Pemberton has been better and he's more than matched by the rest of the cast. This is a very rewarding and interesting episode which probably deserved a bit more love than it received upon transmission.

MERRY CHRISTMAS, MR BEAN (1992)

Merry Christmas, Mr. Bean is a festive edition of the popular comedy show featuring Rowan Atkinson as the childlike Mr Bean - a sort of British version of Pee-Wee Herman. This is a fantastic Christmas episode where Mr Bean partakes in some Christmas shopping and then prepares for Christmas Day - where his girlfriend Irma (Matilda Ziegler) is due for dinner.

I love the Christmas Eve scenes the most in this episode as Mr Bean excitedly prepares for the big day in his little bedsit flat. There is just something very cosy about these scenes and Bean's amazing enthusiasm for Christmas is quite charming. There's a classic moment where some children knock on the door and sing a carol for Mr Bean - who settles back to enjoy this heartwarming rendition of Away in a Manger. When they are finished Bean walks over with a box of chocolates and we presume he is going to give the children some but he simply slams the door on them instead!

I love too how Bean is so excited to wake up on Christmas morning he literally starts jumping and hopping in excitement! There are further capers with Bean getting his head stuck in a turkey (a gag that Friends blatantly ripped off) and an unusually powerful cracker.

Merry Christmas, Mr. Bean is a funny and delightful festive episode and it wouldn't quite be Christmas without a viewing of this great seasonal special.

THE MESSIAH ON MOTT STREET (1971)

"Good evening. Of course you're all here by invitation, but don't let it disturb you if these paintings, per se, don't happen to be your thing. These are rather special paintings, the kind of hangings generally put up with a noose. This painting, for example, is of a rather special world, what has become perpetuated in the language as the ghetto--that dismal realm of pushcarts and poverty where hopes are stamped down like dirty shoes on snow. Death is a commonplace visitor to these somber alleys... but occasionally someone else visits. Our painting is called The Messiah on Mott Street, and this place, should you not already know it, is the Night Gallery."

The Messiah on Mott Street is a segment in a 1971 episode of the anthology show Night Gallery. It was directed by Don Taylor and written by Rod Serling. There has never been anything quite like Night Gallery on television. An anthology in the true sense of the word (until that third season at least). Psychedelic, Gothic, anachronistic, futuristic, high brow, low brow, and all points between, impeccably framed by the great Rod Serling as the curator in an eerie and surreal art gallery unveiling kitsch macabre paintings (by Tom Wright) relating to each story he introduced.

The Messiah on Mott Street is Serling on top form and an example of how great Night Gallery could be at its best. It's Christmas Eve on Manhattan's Lower East Side. In his threadbare and freezing apartment elderly Abraham Goldman (Edward G Robinson) is close to death. He has refused to check into a hospital and is keeping himself alive through will and determination despite what he believes to be the presence of the "Angel of Death" in his room.

Goldman is worried that his grandson Mikey (Ricky Powell) will be put in a foster home if he dies. He is also convinced that

the Messiah will arrive soon and save him. "He's a messenger
from God. Any moment he will appear, looming big and black
against the sky, striking down our enemies and lifting us up to
health and wealth and heavenly contentment." Mikey decides
to go out on the snow frosted streets and look for the Messiah
himself. Will he find him?

This is an unashamedly sentimental and sweet Christmas tale
that can't fail to charm the viewer. Serling and Taylor had
produced the first season classic They're Tearing Down Tom
Riley's Bar and while The Messiah on Mott Street has less bite
it is one of the highlights of the second series. Edward G
Robinson is absolutely brilliant as Goldman, acting his socks
off in every scene, and a fine supporting cast includes Yapphet
Kotto and Tony Roberts. This is one of the best casts in any
Night Gallery episode.

This unusual and offbeat meditation on miracles and faith is
heartwarming stuff with some enjoyably Serling-esque
dialogue. "Who's in here? I know who it is. I know who it is, I
tell you. I have a message for you, you snuffer out of candles,
you wholesaler in the coffin business. I know who you are! And
your unseen face, I tell you, I'm not ready for the Angel of
Death. You I'm not ready for you. Take that back to the
cemetery.

"My pulse still beats, my eyes still see. The flesh still warm,
and my heart... you mumzer from a mausoleum, my heart still
loves! What? Peace, you offer me. You can have that peace,
peace of the grave. No, no thank you. Rest? No cares? Well, I'll
take the cares and the woes and the aggravation, and yes, and
the pain. Listen, Angel! Go down to Argentina, look for Hitler.
Goldman is not ready! My child is out there, the son of my son,
the thing I love. Would I be able to caress him and fondle him
and love him, lying in a box?" The Messiah on Mott Street is
one of the must watch segments in Night Gallery and up there
at the top table with Silent Snow Secret Snow and a select few.

METROPOLITAN (1990)

Metropolitan is the debut film by director and screenwriter Whit Stillman and was released in 1990. The film concerns a group of rich young New York socialites during the debutante season. Into this world arrives Tom Townsend (Edward Clements), a less well heeled Princeton student who is allowed to enter this wealthy 'Rat Pack' after a mix-up over a taxi. We follow these socialites through various parties and encounters as they ponder life, literature, the universe, and also perhaps the most important question that faces people like this. Have they been born into a tradition that already belongs to the past?

This is most assuredly a Christmas movie because it takes place during 'Christmas vacation' and Christmas decorations are visible in many scenes. Metropolitan is a very smart and likeable film where nothing much happens but the dialogue is so enjoyable you don't really care. The film feels like it was written with cultural touchstones like Scott Fitzgerald and Salinger in mind. One scene in particular debates whether or not a particular character is a phony and we all know which literary character loved to call people this.

You don't really have to know too much about preppie rich kids in New York (because, let's be honest, the vast majority of us have no experience of this sort of world!) to enjoy Metropolitan. This is just a clever and gently amusing film that feels like a love letter to another age. What makes the film especially likeable is the fact that these characters know that their little world is not what you might call normal. They are dinosaurs who belong to another age. But they carry on because what else are they supposed to do other than dress up in tuxedos and go to swanky parties? They have no idea themselves. This is a small film but stylishly helmed and one where the dialogue is the star. Metropolitan feels like the sort of film that Woody Allen might have made if he'd been born into a rich family on the Upper East Side.

MICKEY'S CHRISTMAS CAROL (1983)

Mickey's Christmas Carol was directed by Burny Mattinson and was the first thetrical cartoon to feature Mickey Mouse for over thirty years. Happily, this cartoon served as a finme comeback movie for this mouse icon. You get exactly what the title promises here with Scrooge McDuck (voiced by Alan Young) as Ebenezer Scrooge and a cosy Disney family friendly whirl through this famous story.

Mickey Mouse is Bob Cratchit and a host of famous cartoon characters, from Donald Duck to Jiminy Cricket also feature in the story. Your tolerance for this cartoon may depend on your fondness for Scrooge McDuck but you'd have to have a heart of stone not to get into the spirit of things and this is a perfectly enjoyable and likeable cartoon version of the story.

The film runs to about half an hour so the cartoon isn't long enough to have any lulls or overtly talky sections. Even kids with short attention spans should get through this one just fine and have a good time. The real star of this film is the cosy and very colourful animation. Despite the nature of the story this cartoon exudes warmth and festive cheer. There are some laughs too and plenty of fun - especially if you love these Disney characters. If you had one quibble it might be that, despite the story, there never quite seems to be enough of Mickey Mouse as Bob but Mickey's Christmas Carol is still good seasonal animated fun for young and old alike.

A MIDNIGHT CLEAR (1992)

A Midnight Clear was directed by Keith Gordon. The film takes place during the early days of the Battle of the Bulge. A small group of American soldiers are offered a Christmas truce by a platoon of German soldiers who wish to surrender. But will things go according to plan? The Battle of the Bulge is also known as the Ardennes Offensive. This was the last major German offensive of World War 2 and took place close to Christmas in 1944. The ambitious aim of the offensive was to capture the port of Antwerp in Belgium and split the American and British forces. Hitler believed that the Allies would lose their appetite for war as a consequence of the Ardennes Offensive and it would then allow him to transfer men and tanks to the east where they were badly needed to fight the Soviet Union.

But with the Germans lacking experienced battle hardened soldiers and desperately short of fuel for tanks and vehicles, the offensive quickly petered out and fell hopelessly short of expectations. All it did was shorten the war because German armies in the west were now even weaker after the losses in men and tanks. However, in the initial days of the invasion the thinly spread American soldiers had a tough time because an attack was not expected and so the Germans had the element of surprise.

A Midnight Clear doesn't seem to be a terribly well known film - which is a shame really as it is an excellent drama which deals with the tragedy of war. The soldiers on both sides know that the war is nearing some sort of conclusion but they have no idea if they will survive long enough to see peace. There was something incredibly poignant about this battle as it took place in the period running up to Christmas. Christmas is a time of peace, joy, and family but these soldiers are trapped in a dangerous forest as the war
drags on into another year.

There's a really good cast in this film with Ethan Hawke, Gary Sinise, Kevin Dillon, Peter Berg, among others. One of the great things about this film is that it isn't an overblown Hollywood war film but more small scale and personal. The wintry snow glazed backdrops give the film a haunting atmosphere. You wouldn't quite say this was a classic but it is

an impressive little drama and one of the more interesting
World War 2 themed films of fairly recent (if you can call 1992
recent) memory.

MIRACLE ON 34th STREET (1947)

Miracle on 34th Street is an Oscar winning Christmas classic
directed by George Seaton. The story concerns Kris Kringle
(Edmund Gwenn) - a man who ends up as a Macy's
department store Santa in New York after the original Santa
turned up drunk. Here's the thing though. Kringle seems to
have an uncanny knack of performing what you might describe
as miracles. Could it be that he really is Father Christmas?

This is a charming film and probably ranks only second to It's
a Wonderful Life when it comes to Christmas classics from Old
Hollywood. Gwenn is terrific as Kringle and look out for
Natalie Wood in her child acting days. There are many
heartwarming scenes in the film - especially early on when
Kringle seems to be performing some Santa related miracles.
Naturally though, Kringle's acts are not believed by everyone.

One of the themes of this film is how adults tend to have
closed minds when it comes to anything outside the realm of
crushing reality. Children however are a different breed. They
still have imaginations where anything is possible. One of the
great things about this film too is that it was shot on location
in New York. They didn't just shoot on a set in Hollywood and
pretend it was New York. This gives the film a nice authentic
New York atmosphere and it goes without saying that the
Christmas atmosphere is absolutely fantastic. There isn't
anything to dislike about this film. It is sentimental without
ladling on the treacle too much and the cast is fantastic. This is
a film fully deserving of its status as a Christmas classic.

MISTER MAGOO'S CHRISTMAS CAROL (1962)

This is a 53 minute animated version of A Christmas Carol with the short-sighted curmudgeon Mister Maggo (voiced by jim Backus) as Ebenezer Scrooge and Jack Cassidy as the voice of Bob Cratchit. What's not to like about that? The story is framed by this being a Broadway show and there are plenty of laughs along the way and a raft of nice songs. The animation is functional but cosy and it serves as a pretty good version (in fact, the ghosts are rather scary when they arrive) of the famous story.

This is longer than some of the other animated versions of A Christmas Carol but it never feels unduly padded or overlong and is consistently amusing and engaging. Mister Maggo's Christmas Carol is a surprisingly straight adaptation of the story too and quite faithful and effective. It goes without saying also that Mister Maggo makes a wonderful fit for the persona of Ebenezer Scrooge. This is one of those old Christmas cartoons that deserves to be shown a lot more these days than it actually is. By the way, you should try and make you watch the full version of this as an edited version exists due to the fact that some stations cut out the Broadway framing sequences in order to make more room for commercials. I rather like the Broadway stuff myself.

THE MUPPET CHRISTMAS CAROL (1992)

Believe it not, despite its status as a Christmas classic today, The Muppet Christmas Carol was a box-office flop and got fairly lukewarm reviews when it was first released in 1992. That seems hard to believe doesn't it? These days it just wouldn't feel like Christmas without this movie on TV over the festive period. The film has grown in stature over the decades and is now regarded to be arguably the finest hour of the Muppets when it comes to their cinema outings. The Muppet films can be a trifle hit or miss but this one, obviously aided by the fact that it is an adaptation of a famous story, is much more consistent.

There's not too much to dislike here. Gonzo as Charles Dickens narrating the tale, Kermit and Miss Piggy as Mr and Mrs Cratchit, Statler and Waldorf as Jacob and Robert Marley, and so on. For my money the funniest character in the film is Gonzo's assistant Rizzo the Rat. I like the moment where he is used as a cloth to wipe a frosty window!

Last but by no means least we Michael Caine as Scrooge. Caine's straight performance gives the film some gravitas and he makes a good anchor around which the Muppet hijinks take place.

This is a surprisingly faithful rendition of this famous story and the sets and Victorian atmosphere are excellent. Critics seemed somewhat unimpressed by the songs in the film when it came out but I find them perfectly fine and enjoyable. The film is occasionally a trifle talky for kids but you are never too far away from a song or some funny stuff involving the Muppets. What makes this film work is that it has a sincerity and clarity of purpose. It wants to give us a good adaption of A Christmas Carol - only with Muppets! In this aim it succeeds admirably.

The Muppet Christmas Carol is not only a terrific version of A Christmas Carol it is also a terrific Muppet movie.

NATIONAL LAMPOON'S CHRISTMAS VACATION (1989)

The Griswolds are a fictional family who first featured in the 1983 hit comedy film National Lampoon's Vacation. Chevy Chase plays the head of the family, the accident prone Clark Griswold. The sequel, National Lampoon's European Vacation, came out in 1985. The Griswolds returned in 1989's National Lampoon's Christmas Vacation, and then in 1997's Vegas Vacation. For my money at least, the best of these films is National Lampoon's Christmas Vacation.

Christmas Vacation, as one would expect, is dripping in festive residue and it is also a really funny film. This film was directed by Jeremiah S. Chechik and written by John Hughes. The basic premise of the film is that Clark wants to give his family the perfect Christmas - like the ones he remembers enjoying with his family as a child. Matters are complicated though by the arrival of a large gaggle of annoying relatives and - as usual - everything going wrong for the accident prone Clark.

There's a terrific cast here around Chase and Beverly D'Angelo (as Clark's long suffering but supportive wife Ellen) with E. G. Marshall, Doris Roberts, Julia Louis-Dreyfus, William Hickey, and Mae Questel. The daughter Audrey Griswold is played by Juliette Lewis just prior to her breakout roles in Cape Fear and Husbands and Wives and the son Russ is played by future Big Bang Theory star Johnny Galecki.

National Lampoon's Christmas Vacation has plenty of memorable moments - like Clark's attempt to have a preposterously elaborate Christmas light display. I also love the moment where he carves the turkey. It wouldn't be a Vacation film without Randy Quaid as cousin Eddie and Eddie naturally arrives with his rather obstreperous family to add to the festive chaos. Quaid is, as usual, a big scene stealer in this movie. National Lampoon's Christmas Vacation only threatens to veer off course in a slightly tiresome subplot where Clark, annoyed that his Xmas work bonus hasn't arrived (he was banking on the money to build a swimming pool), kidnaps his boss.

This quibble aside though, Christmas Vacation is cosy, full of Christmas atmosphere, and fitfully amusing. This is a great film to watch in the build up to Christmas. People sometimes tend to be a bit sniffy about this film but I think National Lampoon's Christmas Vacation is a lot of fun. It's also rather unique to have a movie in this franchise where the Griswolds don't actually go anywhere and just stay at home!

THE NIGHTMARE BEFORE CHRISTMAS (1993)

The Nightmare Before Christmas is an animated film directed by Henry Selick. The story was by Tim Burton - who also produced the film. The film revolves around Halloween World - a place generally run by Jack Skellington. Jack, as his name implies, resembles a skeleton and is the Pumpkin King. One day, Jack becomes aware of the existence of other fantasy worlds which have different themes. He is fascinated in particular by the discovery of a Christmas themed world. Jack has no idea what Christmas is but decides that in addition to being in charge of Halloween he should have a bash at doing Christmas too. To this end he kidnaps Santa but his schemes turn out to be a lot more complicated than he expected.

The Nightmare Before Christmas is something different from your usual bog standard Hollywood animated film and children should enjoy the spooky and weird trappings on offer here. The story is nothing to write home about but the film is visually arresting and always enjoyable to look at. What is especially effective is the way that it deploys different styles of animation to convey different places and moods.

For the most part it's rather like a live pop-up book and the stop-motion (a technique which harkens back to old masters like Ray Harryhausen) is great. There's a fine cast of voice actors too led by Chris Sarandon and Catherine O'Hara. The Nightmare Before Christmas is one of those rare animated films that children should love but it won't leave adults bored if they have to sit through it too. If you are are looking for a Christmas animated film which offers something a bit different from the norm then The Nightmare Before Christmas will provide that in spades.

THE NIGHT OF THE HUNTER (1955)

The Night of the Hunter is a 1955 thriller directed by Charles Laughton. Yes, this film does have a Christmas theme so certainly qualifies for our list. Robert Mitchum is unforgettable in this film as Reverend Harry Powell. Powell is a preacher who marries Willa Harper (Shelly Winters) but he has a dark secret. Powell is really a serial killer who kills women for their money.

Powell had shared a cell with Willa's late husband Ben and learned that Ben has $10,000 stashed away from a robbery. Ben said that his children knew where the money was but he told them never to reveal this location to anyone. Well, Powell naturally decides that if he bumps off Willa then he can get the children to reveal where the money is and he will do literally anything to achieve his goals.

The Night of the Hunter is an amazingly gripping and atmospheric thriller with a terrifying performance by Mitchum. Oddly, this film actually got poor reviews when it came out but then (happily) went on to be regarded as something of a classic. There is one tremendously haunting and unforgettable shot in this film where a body, complete with flowing hair, is shown at the bottom of a river. It's great stuff and a shame really that Laughton never directed another film. Harry Powell is truly one of the most terrifying villains in film history.

NIGHT OF THE MEEK (1960)

"This is Mr Henry Corwin, normally unemployed, who once a year takes the lead role in the uniquely popular American institute, that of department-store Santa Claus in a road company version of 'The Night Before Christmas.' But in just a moment Mr Henry Corwin, ersatz Santa Claus, will enter a strange kind of North Pole which is one part the wondrous spirit of Christmas and one part the magic that can only be found in the Twilight Zone."

Might of the Meek is a 1960 episode of The Twilight Zone. It was directed by Jack Smight and written by Rod Serling. In Night of the Meek, a drunken department store Santa named Henry Corwin (Art Carney) is fired from his job for always being sozzled. He drowns his sorrows in the nearest bar (still wearing his tatty Santa suit) and then finds a strange bag that can magically dispense any gift he wants. Now invested with the real powers of Santa, Corwin decides to spread as much joy and generosity as he can with this magical find...

Night of the Meek was one of Rod Serling's favourite Twilight Zones and he apparently used to screen it at Christmas for his friends and family. It's certainly a nice episode and a pleasant experience but it does become a trifle cloying and sentimental at times. Still, I suppose you'd have to be a real life Scrooge to complain abut this one too much. It's just a nice charming Christmas yarn where a man gets a chance to bring some magical Christmas spirit into the lives of 'hopeless and dreamless'.

It's a shame really that Night of the Meek is one of the dreaded videotape episodes because the seasonal sets are very nice and cosy and definitely would have been even better if shot on film. Night of the Meek is probably a little overrated in the Twilight Zone canon but it is generally an enjoyable experience and Art Carney is very good as our unexpected Christmas hero. This is somewhat saccharine and obvious but you'd have to have a heart of stone not to enjoy Night of the Meek. One to watch on Christmas Eve.

ON HER MAJESTY'S SECRET SERVICE (1969)

On Her Majesty's Secret Service, the first Bond film not to feature Sean Connery, is often written about as if it was a dreadful failure but this was not the case. Sure, audiences at the time unavoidably missed Sean Connery but the film made some money and is now felt by many fans (and I would include myself among them) to be the best James Bond movie ever made. It should be noted that Connery probably wouldn't have mustered much enthusiasm for OHMSS even if he had somehow been lured back. Besides, one of the strengths of the film was that Lazenby's youth and inexperience gave him a vulnerability which wouldn't have been so believable if conveyed by Connery's Bond. Oddly enough, Lazenby, though an inferior actor, actually suited the more human story of OHMSS more than Connery.

Strangely, it's not that difficult to watch OHMSS and just accept this is still Connery's Bond only with a different actor - and the film is determined to run with that concept, even linking the title sequence into the Connery films. Lazenby was chosen because of his physical similarities to Connery. As with Connery, Lazenby was also believably tough and had a rough and ready sort of quality. After George Lazenby declined an invitation to return as James Bond in Diamonds Are Forever, he was frozen as the 'one-off Bond' and it was often wrongly assumed that both Lazenby and OHMSS had been a failure. Over time though, the strengths of the film have been rightly acknowledged.

The spectacular Alpine locations, the supporting cast of Diana Rigg and Telly Savalas, the fantastic action sequences, and the decision to stick closely to Ian Fleming's original novel. This is the only Bond film too to have scenes set around Christmas and even Christmas songs. The most faithful, human, and best James Bond film ever made, On Her Majesty's Secret Service never quite got the credit it deserved, then or now. Never before or again would a James Bond film have such an acute sense of style right down to the costumes.

Bond relies on his own wits in this film more than others. Q, who only appears at the end, does not supply a host of gadgets to save 007's life. That alone was radical after the jet-pack and ejector-seat era of Connery. There are countless moments that mark OHMSS as a special entry in the series. The helicopter going up to Piz Gloria. The original ski-chase. Bond actually doing some detective work and reflecting on past adventures because, as it should be, this is supposed to be the same character as before. Tracey being dragged away in the snow as Bond looks out of the window in M's office. And Diana Rigg who can probably never be equalled as the female lead.

Lazenby's fight scenes are the best in the series too. This is one James Bond who really can fight his way out of trouble. In the course of this film Lazenby is tough, petulant, arrogant, vulnerable, and an expense account snob. He IS James Bond. Always in the middle of the action, Lazenby looks the part and shrewdly surrounded by good actors and tight-editing makes for, in my opinion, an exciting younger Bond.

PROMETHEUS (2012)

Yes, Ridley Scott's Prometheus is set at Christmas. There is even a Christmas tree on the spaceship! This is a flawed film but an interesting one. Prometheus is set in the late 21st century and centres on the crew of the spaceship Prometheus as it follows a star map discovered among the artifacts of several ancient Earth cultures. Seeking the origins of humanity, the crew arrives on LV-223, a distant moon, and discovers a threat that could cause the extinction of the human species...

The film starts with an albino alien humanoid creating life on Earth with a black goo. Well, it could be Earth. "That could be anywhere," said Ridley Scott. "That could be a planet anywhere. All he's doing is acting as a gardener in space. And the plant life, in fact, is the disintegration of himself." The humanoid sacrifices himself and falls into a waterfall. This is an 'Engineer' - the fossilised creature in Alien in the huge chair that looked like a giant elephant. By revealing that these mysterious alien creatures really look like bald albino human bodybuilders and were simply wearing giant suits, the film conclusively proves that less is more and more is less. Leave them mysterious I say. All the wonderful mystery of the space jockey scene in Alien is ruined. The Lovecraftian theme that the universe is a strange and unfathomable place. A place that we can't ever truly understand. The space jockey was compelling because we had no idea what it was.

The crew in Prometheus don't make for a very memorable or convincing cast of characters despite the big names enticed into appearing in the film. Noomi Rapace is an absolute blank as archaeologist Elizabeth Shaw and Charlize Theron is underused as the cold Weyland Corporation employee Vickers. Vickers is so bad tempered and snooty to everyone you wonder why anyone would put up with her. They must be getting an awful lot of money to resist the urge to throw her overboard. There is a twist involving Vickers that partly explains her character but all the same it isn't completely satisfying.

Theron was originally going to play Shaw but she was unavailable because of the long production of Mad Max: Fury Road. When she was free again she joined Prometheus in the lesser role of Vickers. It's a shame that the original plan didn't go ahead because Theron is a much stronger presence than Rapace as an actress and arguably would have made a better anchor for the film to revolve around. Logan Marshall-Green is forgettable as Shaw's doomed love interest Charlie Holloway and Idris Elba feels rather wasted as the Janek, the captain. Elba stays in the ship and is required to talk like an old sailor.

Janek doesn't show too much concern when a couple of characters are trapped in a cave system for the night. Prometheus is strange in this way. Characters often act in an inexplicable and strange fashion. Nothing ever quite makes any sense. The only great performance in the film comes from Michael Fassbender as the android David. The start of the space voyage consists entirely of David alone as the crew are in hypersleep. We see David style his hair, eat, play basketball on a bike, and watch Lawrence of Arabia. These scenes of David alone in the ship are wonderful and evoke the opening scenes of Alien when Scott's camera roamed the empty Nostromo with haunting music.

Ridley Scott seems more interested in the artificial intelligence element of the story than treading over old ground (facehuggers/xenomorphs etc) so it is just as well that Fassbender is here to play this part of the story. Prometheus would be much more of a slog and less memorable without Fassbender's effortlessly charismatic performance. Prometheus doesn't have that Planet of the Vampires desolate mist shrouded atmosphere we associate with the Alien franchise. These characters don't look like they are on an alien world. They look like they are in Iceland! There are new creatures in the film to torment the crew like alien snakes and octopus type entities. The obvious CGI makes them artificial and not very memorable.

One effective sequence in Prometheus though has Shaw performing self surgery using a Med Pod (an automated medical device) after being impregnated with an alien nasty. This scene was conceived by Spaihts in his original treatment. The biggest complaint about Prometheus is the stupidity of the characters. Trying to pet a vicious looking alien snake, getting lost in caves despite mapping them on a computer, trying to outrun a falling spaceship when it would be easier to just move to the side. What's going on with Sean Harris as the stupid thuggish geologist Fifield? Here he is on the scientific jaunt of a lifetime and he acts like a schoolboy who's been forced to go to school on a rainy Monday morning.

Having mentioned much in the film that doesn't work, what are the merits of Prometheus aside from Michael Fassbender's superlative performance? One would have to admit that - while the film is frustrating in places and doesn't quite mesh as a whole - it is thrilling at times to a see a science fiction picture made with this degree of craft and money again. Ridley Scott can still beautifully capture spellbinding images and the film often looks terrific. The scene where the characters are caught in a violent storm as they try to get back to the ship is superbly orchestrated. Perhaps the most magical sequence in Prometheus comes when David activates a holographic device of the Engineers. Prometheus is a film of great images and moments that never quite manage to form a complete and satisfying film.

One could argue that the baggage of Alien doesn't really do the film any favours. With a few tweaks this could have been an original sci-fi film that had nothing to do with the Alien series and might be thought of more fondly as a consequence. The ideas in the film about the search for a creator and David's growing resentment of humans (to his great disappointment, David knows exactly who created him) are interesting but somewhat negated by some vague characters and a few baffling decisions in the script. It's typical of this film that when they introduce Weyland, the ancient billionaire founder and CEO of Weyland Corp, he's played by Guy Pearce in ridiculous hokey old age make-up. Ultimately, the predictable fate of Prometheus was a good looking film with an iffy screenplay that couldn't live up to Alien but had some pretty visuals. Some liked it and others didn't.

RARE EXPORTS: A CHRISTMAS TALE (2010)

Rare Exports: A Christmas Tale is a Finnish horror film directed by Jalmari Helander. The film was inspired by a short film the director made in 2003. Rare Exports: A Christmas Tale takes place in Korvatunturi (a fell in Lapland, on the border between Finland and Russia) where a foreign drilling research team attract the attention of some local boys because of their activity on a mountain.

The research team seem to have dug up something very ancient - and as it transpires - something very dangerous. The research team have dug up Joulupukki, a sinister figure in Northern European folklore who punishes badly behaved children. Rare Exports: A Christmas Tale has a beautiful ice glazed backdrop and is an inventive horror take on an alternative sort of origin tale for Santa. The film seems to be quite inspired by John Carpenter's The Thing - which is obviously a plus.

Both movies have a similar concept of ordinary people battling an unfathomable horror in an isolated location. Rare Exports: A Christmas Tale is beautifully shot with some gore and black humour. The film also has an ecological subtext in that the companies looking for ways to exploit this beautiful wilderness only serve to unleash something awful. The characters in the film are vivid and some of the set-pieces are very well staged. This is an unusual sort of film and difficult to describe but anyone who enjoys Christmas themed horror films which involve folklore should find Rare Exports a highly satisfying experience.

ROCKY IV (1985)

The fourth Rocky is by some distance the daftest in the series but I suppose you could qualify this as a guilty pleasure. Sly Stallone directed this one again. Rocky IV feels less like a proper film than the previous entries and doesn't have much of a plot. It is padded out by music montages and sometimes feels more like a pop video than a movie. It is fun though in a silly 1980s sort of way.

In the film Rocky's friend (and old rival) Apollo Creed decides to come out of retirement to fight an exhibition bout with a hulking Soviet boxer named Ivan Drago (Dolph Lundgren). Drago clearly doesn't understand the concept of an exhibition bout though because he batters Creed so badly that Apollo dies. Rocky decides to get revenge in the ring but this comes with a condition. Drago's people tell Rocky that if he wants to fight Drago the bout must occur in the Soviet Union on Christmas Day!

You can tell this isn't going to be the realistic of movies early on when Paulie is given a talking robot for his birthday! There's a lot of silly stuff in Rocky IV but the montages are fun and you get James Brown singing at Apollo's fight. The climactic battle between Rocky and Drago is preposterous but well staged and entertaining. Rocky's mumbling monologue at the end though is probably something the film could have lived without. The franchise would only really get back on track with the excellent (and much later) Rocky Balboa but if you want to park your brain in neutral and want undemanding boxing themed fun with a very 1980s atmosphere and soundtrack then Rocky IV will provide that.

ROCKY V (1990)

The fifth go around for Rocky brought back the original Rocky director John G Avildsen in an attempt to go back to basics and make a more grounded sort of Rocky film more in line with the first one.

The film has Rocky back from Russia after his fight with Ivan Drago. Life turns sour for our hero when he learns his brother-in-law Paulie (Burt Young) has frittered his fortune away on a bad real estate deal. Rocky is bankrupt but can't box anymore because of brain damage he suffered in his career. Rocky is forced to move back to his old neighbourhood and Adrian (Talia Shire) gets her old pet shop job again. Rocky finds a new purpose in life though when he takes a young fighter named Tommy Gunn under his wing. This makes Rocky's son (played by Sage Stallone) rather jealous.

Stallone's people left no stone unturned looking for someone to play Tommy Gunn and came up with what appeared to be the perfect candidate. Tommy Morrison was a real life 21 year-old heavyweight prospect from Arkansas. Morrison was 6'2, muscled, a puncher (famed for his deadly left-hook) with a crowd pleasing style, blonde, good looking, and articulate. Morrison's handlers even came up with a great marketing gimmick by (dubiously) claiming he was related to John Wayne - thus earning him his nickname 'Duke'. Morrison was cast as Tommy Gunn and saw his profile go through the roof. Stallone even shot footage at some of Morrison's real fights to use in Rocky V.

Morrison loved making Rocky V and said it was a great experience. His plan was to become the world heavyweight champion and then once his boxing career had run its course he would go back to acting again. Sadly, Morrison's plans never came to fruition on either of those two fronts. Morrison was passable enough though in Rocky V. He's obviously more convincing in the boxing scenes than he is with dialogue (especially when Stallone's script abruptly - and not entirely convincingly - turns Tommy Gunn into an angry villain who hates Rocky and wants to go off with some Don King style loudmouth) but he had the potential to get better and do more movies.

Rocky V is perfectly watchable although the plot seems rather contrived. It's a little silly the way that Rocky even takes to wearing his old leather jacket and hat from the first film again. Still, I suppose real life is full of boxers who lost their fortune and ended up back where they started. It's a familiar story when it comes to the sweet science. The film riffs a lot on real life boxing politics and double dealing when Tommy Gunn is enticed away from Rocky by the sleazy motor mouthed promoter George Washington Duke (Richard Grant). Duke is basically Don King and the story is clearly inspired by King stealing Mike Tyson from his manager Bill Cayton and his trainer Kevin Rooney.

Sly's son Sage plays his son in the film and although he is no great shakes as an actor the scenes are poignant now given the tragic early death of Sage. Real life boxer Tommy Morrison (also sadly no longer with us) is decent enough as Tommy Gunn given that he wasn't a real actor. The fight scenes in the film are quite good because other real life boxers like Mike Williams play fighters in the film.

What really seemed to sink Rocky V for most people I suspect is the fact that this is the only Rocky film that doesn't climax with a boxing match. It ends with a street brawl in an alley between Rocky and his estranged and angry former pupil. This fight is well staged but - all the same - doesn't have the appeal or excitement of seeing Rocky in the ring. Rocky V is not flat out terrible but one could probably argue that it is a rather disappointing sequel.

Rocky V is an interesting attempt to go back to basics and largely works but it does get a bit silly when Tommy abruptly turns into a villain. The Rocky franchise would be much better served by the later Rocky Balboa and the Creed spin-off movies. Anyway, why am I babbling on about Rocky V in a book about Christmas movies? Well, the final street fight between Rocky and Tommy clearly takes place at Christmas!

RUDOLF THE RED-NOSED REINDEER (1964)

Rudolph the Red-Nosed Reindeer is a beloved television animated film based on the Johnny Marks song of the same name. The film features the adventures of the title character, who, amongst other capers, encounters the Abominable Snow Monster and the Island of Misfit Toys. This film has a very cosy and comforting winter Christmas atmosphere with a blanket of white snow framing the action.

What is especially charming about this film too is that it uses stop-motion animation - a technique which is something of a lost art these days. From a modern vantage point, where we are deluged with endless state of the art CGI cartoons and movies, the old fashioned stop-motion animation in Rudolph the Red-Nosed Reindeer is very enjoyable and refreshing. Not only that but it somehow imbues the characters with real personality and charm.

This is reputedly the longest running Christmas special in the United States and for many viewers it just wouldn't be Christmas without a viewing of Rudolph the Red-Nosed Reindeer. This is definitely a cartoon that should keep younger kids happy on Christmas Day morning while you attend to the dinner and do a few other tasks.

SANTA CLAUS CONQUERS THE MARTIANS (1964)

Santa Claus Conquers the Martians is a 1964 children's sci-fi film directed by Nicholas Webster. In the film a family of Martians get fed up that their children keep watch Earth's television shows and fear that Martian life is too regimented in comparison to Earth. So they decide to kidnap Santa Claus so that Martian children can have more fun. Not all the Martians are happy about this though so tension soon arises. Oh, and a couple of Earth kids also end up being kidnapped. Or something like that. You didn't really expect a coherent plot in a film called Santa Claus Conquers the Martians anyway did you?

Santa Claus Conquers the Martians is generally considered to be one of the worst films ever made and as such has earned a mildly cultish status. It's sort of like Robot Monster. Robot Monster, by any logical criteria is a dreadful film but it is actually a lot of fun too by dint of being so laughable. Santa Claus Conquers the Martians sort of works along the same lines. This movie, I gather, got a lot of retrospective fame when it was mocked on Mystery Science theater 3000. Santa Claus Conquers the Martians feels like one of those movies that was genetically engineered in a lab purely for the purposes of Mystery Science theater 3000!

The film is cheesy, badly acted, and has a ridiculous plot. It is though enjoyably garish and colourful and the costumes are so preposterous they can't help but make you laugh. Santa Claus Conquers the Martians is absolutely ridiculous but it is sort of charming too in a so bad it's watchable sort of way. Kids would probably have a good time with this film and adults will get a laugh out of it too. Despite its palpable naffness, Santa Claus Conquers the Martians is actually good fun if you approach it in the right frame of mind. I think everyone should watch this film at least once in their lives at Christmas. There is nothing else quite like it.

SANTA CLAUS: THE MOVIE (1985)

Santa Claus: The Movie is a debatable entry on this list because it got terrible reviews and is not regarded to be a very good film at all. It's certainly no Christmas classic that's for sure but time and nostalgia has lent the film a certain cheesy sort of charm and it's an experience if nothing else. Santa Claus: The Movie is one of those films which is more popular with audiences today than it ever was with critics at the time.

Most of us have probably stumbled across this movie on television at Christmas. In fact, although the film is rather disappointing on the whole, it STILL wouldn't quite be Christmas without Santa Claus: The Movie playing on television during the festive season at least once! This film was made by the father-and-son production team of Alexander and Ilya Salkind. The Salkinds were the producers behind the Christopher Reeve Superman movies. A lot of the special effects people who worked on the Superman and James Bond movies worked on Santa Claus: The Movie and the film was directed by Jeannot Szwarc (who previously directed the Supergirl movie for the Salkinds).

Santa Claus: The Movie had a huge budget and was quite hyped at the time but it turned out to be a big box-office dud. Anyway, what is the plot of Santa Claus: The Movie? The plot concerns Dudley Moore as Patch, an elf who works for Santa (David Huddleston). When one of Patch's inventions to speed up the production of gifts goes a bit haywire he ends up exiled in New York where he is manipulated by the heartless toymaker B.Z (John Lithgow). Needless to say, all will turn out fine in the end.

The first half of this film is definitely better than the second half and it becomes something of a slog to get through at times but it does generate a sense of magic and wonder in its best moments and the special effects and production design are good for the era. Dudley Moore is likeable and Huddleston makes a decent enough Santa. Lithgow is given a fairly thankless role as the sneering villain but you do get the great Burgess Meredith as the Ancient Elf.

Santa Claus: The Movie is sort of fascinating merely by dint of being so weird and all over the place. It's like the Salkinds came up with the idea of making a film about Father Christmas but could never actually work out what to do in the movie! Despite all of its patent flaws (including some gruesome product placement), Santa Claus: The Movie is certainly a Christmas film you should experience at least once in your life but whether you'd ever return to it again is another question altogether.

A SCANDAL IN BELGRAVIA (2012)

This is an episode of the Sherlock television series with Benedict Cumberbatch. It has scenes set at Christmas so it goes in this book! A Scandal in Belgravia was directed by Paul McGuigan and written by Steven Moffat (based on A Scandal in Bohemia). Mycroft hires Sherlock and John to find compromising photos of a minor royal - which are held on the phone of Irene Adler (Lara Pulver). Adler is a ruthless dominatrix who trades in secret information extracted from her rich and powerful clients. Sherlock obtains Adler's phone but finds it is booby-trapped and requires a code to disarm it. When Adler discovers that the CIA are on her trail, she vanishes and is then apparently killed only to reappear to ask John to get her phone back from Sherlock. Weeks later when the coast is clear, Adler tricks Sherlock into decoding a

message on her phone which she obtained from another client.
She sends the message to Moriarty - who in turn uses it to
negate a British counter-terror operation...

Series two begins with this brilliant and well directed episode
that throws Irene Adler into the mix. Lara Pulver is fine as a
super confident Adler and although Steven Moffat is
sometimes criticised for his writing of women (critics note
how, for example, Russell T Davies tended to write more
sympathetic and believable female characters than Moffat
during their respective stints on Doctor Who) the controversial
scene where Adler greets Sherlock naked when he breaks into
her home is clever because it means Sherlock has no way of
reading her. There are no visual clues for him to get a handle
on her. Pulver was best known for her roles in the BBC shows
Spooks and Robin Hood. Irene Adler is known professionally
as The Woman. She takes pictures of her clients during her job
as protection to make sure her clients don't do anything
unfavourable to her.

Highlights of A Scandal in Belgravia include Sherlock being
taken to Buckingham Palace while not dressed (note how he
deduces where he might be heading by dog hairs on trousers!)
and it's amusing the way Sherlock & John are like little boys at
the palace and can't help but laugh at their situation. It's nice
to see some glee and childish humour from the sometimes
stern Sherlock. Sherlock's mind palace deduction simulation
in the forest makes for a visually arresting and clever
sequence. Sherlock seemingly has a vast database of
information in his head but finding it is rather like someone
having to search through files in a drawer. It requires some
intense concentration and no small amount of patience.

Notice too how Sherlock Holmes' forensic knowledge of
London trains in the books is updated here and he has an
incredible amount of detail at his fingertips about London
planes. These incredible feats of deduction and brainpower
strain credibility but it's believable that Sherlock would have to
study such a thing. He does need to have a vast and extensive

knowledge of the cogs and nuts and bolts of London to be effective in his very singular line of work. Look out for the use of Vatican Cameos - the emergency codeword Sherlock and Watson use to alert one another to imminent danger. The phrase comes from Conan Doyle's original Hound of the Baskervilles story, where Sherlock Holmes refers in passing to the affair of the Vatican Cameos.

There's a touching scene where Sherlock mocks an overdressed Molly for her bag of Christmas gifts and makes fun of the most lavishly wrapped present which he deduces is for someone she loves. But of course, it quickly dawns on him that the present is for him. John is naturally surprised when Sherlock - of all people - offers a sincere apology.
The big cliffhanger from the last episode is dispensed with by use of a Bee Gees ringtone when Moriarty receives an urgent call. It's a slight cop out but we can rest assured that he'll be back.

One interesting thing about this episode is the way the usually unflappable Sherlock is put under more pressure than usual and we see how he reacts. Adler is more or less a match for him in cunning (if not quite brain power) and he doesn't quite know how to react to this. It's rare for him to meet someone that he can't completely read. Sherlock and Irene engage in an amusing battle of wits throughout the story. A Scandal in Belgravia is Sherlock firing on all cylinders. The score by David Arnold and Michael Rice is stellar, the direction is stylish, Cumberbatch has real chemistry with his leading lady, and the plot is precise and interesting - presenting us us with a series of small mysteries to ponder and think about.

The episode concludes as Mycroft tells John that she has been killed by a terrorist group in Pakistan - while in fact she was secretly rescued by Sherlock. This opens the door for Irene to return to the series but - thus far - this return has yet to transpire. It seems like a shame that Irene never returned to the series as she would have made a good recurring foil and vague romantic interest for Sherlock to banter with. Perhaps the limited number of Sherlock episodes nixed this possibility. If it was a more conventional series with ten or so episodes to fill up each season then perhaps she almost certainly have returned. Maybe in the end there simply wasn't room for more of this character what with the Moriarty cliffhangers and the introduction of Mary.

There are, as usual, a large number of little Sherlockian references in this episode that are fun to watch out for. When Sherlock mentions the 'speckled blonde' this is obviously a nod to The Adventure of the Speckled Band. John's blog title 'Sherlock Holmes Baffled' is a reference to the 1900 film of the same name - which was the first time the great detective had appeared onscreen. Moriarty's text message to Mycroft ('Dear me, Mr Holmes. Dear me') is taken from the epilogue of The Valley of Fear. Sherlock's saying that he doesn't take orders from anonymous customers is taken from The Adventure of the Illustrious Client. You may notice too that John's middle name is revealed to be Hamish - which is line with the general lore of the books.

The deerstalker cap makes an appearance here when Sherlock uses it to hide from the media. Naturally this is a rather anachronistic and strange sort of hat for the present day and so it is not completely surprising that Sherlock isn't a great fan of the hat. In this updated Sherlock, the hat is sort of like a 'character' costume that Sherlock occasionally dons to play up to the media image of him. It is not an everyday hat that he would really wear though. There is a reference in this episode to Sherlock deducing that there are 240 different types of tobacco ash. This is taken from The Sign of Four (where Holmes deduces there are 140 different types of tobacco ash).

A Scandal in Belgravia includes a conversation where Sherlock and John discuss the names that John gives their cases. Sherlock suggests the 'belly button murders' and John relies by saying 'the naval treatment'. This is a reference to The Adventure of the Naval Treaty. Sherlock's snooty disdain for John's habit of giving their cases titles also includes a reference to The Adventure of the Greek Interpreter. The thumb in the fridge is a nod to the short story The Adventure of the Engineer's Thumb.

Mark Gatiss as Mycroft is given some funny moments in this episode - like the scene where Mycroft and Sherlock discuss the nature of the photographs that had compromised the minor royal. Or his smile when Molly asks how Sherlock recognised the naked woman in the morgue. While Sherlock was sometimes criticised for making the character too James Bond at times there are some nice economical action scenes in this episode like when Sherlock dispenses with the goons who have roughed up Mrs Hudson. The fact that he identifies vulnerable body parts in his mind text could be a sly reference to the 2009 Sherlock Holmes film.

The scene where Sherlock finally cracks Irene's code is one of the best in any episode of Sherlock. There is some fine acting here and the music serves as the perfect backdrop. Although there is plenty of action in A Scandal in Belgravia it is still a surprisingly good character episode that fleshes out these characters even more from the first season.
It is hard really to come away from A Scandal in Belgravia with too many complaints. This is the show at or near the peak of its powers. This is a very stylish 90 minutes of television with plenty of twists and turns and some sharp and witty dialogue. One could argue that this was, at that point, the best episode of Sherlock to date.

SCROOGE (1951)

1951's Scrooge (known as A Christmas Carol in the United States) was directed by Brian Desmond Hurst and is considered by many to be the definitive version of A Christmas Carol. This is a beautifully made film and the icing on the cake is the peerless character actor Alistair Sim as Scrooge. Sim is still regarded to be the definitive Scrooge by many and one can see why in this film.

One of the interesting things about the film is the way that it lends more focus than usual on Scrooge as a young businessman. We see more of how he turned into the miserable old miser of legend. Oddly, this is another one of those classic Christmas films too which got mixed reviews when it came out! The legend of this film has grown over the years though and it's hard to think of many Christmas themed films which can rival this one.

There's an amazing cast here too with Michael Hordern as Jacob Marley's Ghost, Mervyn Johns as Bob Cratchit, and many more memorable actors. Look out too for a young George Cole and Patrick Macnee and also Hattie Jacques as Mrs. Fezziwig. Sim's spooked reactions to everything around him are wonderful and he really owns this famous role. There is plenty of atmosphere in the film too with the black and white photography and fine music score. As far as Christmas Carol adaptations go this was far from the first (or the last!) but it is generally considered to be the best.

SCROOGE (1970)

"Thank you very much, that's the nicest thing that anyone's ever done for me!" Scrooge, directed by Ronald Neame, is a 1970 musical adaptation of A Christmas Carol with Albert Finney in the title role. I think the songs in this film are destined, for better or worse, to rattle around in my head for all eternity! This was actually the first colour version of this timeless story and the film remains a lot of fun. This will certainly put you in a festive mood if you give it a whirl in the run up to Christmas.

Finney (who was only third choice for the part after Richard Harris and Rex Harrison) was only in his thirties when he played this part and his old age make-up is a trifle on the hokey side but Scrooge is a film to be enjoyed rather than nitpicked. It's a bit camp and cheesy but that's all part of the fun. The film was able to use the sets that had been built for the Oscar winning musical Oliver! so it's a handsome looking production with a fine period atmosphere.

Finney's eccentric performance might not be to all tastes but he's good value for money and always entertaining as this legendary miser. There's a fine cast of British thespians around Finney too with Alec Guinness as Jacob Marley, Kenneth More as the Ghost of Christmas Present, and Edith Evans as Ghost of Christmas Past. There are a host of familar faces too in the supporting cast like Anton Rodgers, Gordon Jackson, Roy Kinnear, and Geoffrey Bayldon. Scrooge doesn't quite seem to have become what you might describe as a classic but it got decent enough reviews and seems to be fondly remembered these days. This is good undemanding Christmas fun - especially if you like musicals.

SEASONS OF BELIEF (1986)

This is a season three episode from the cheap and cheerful eighties horror anthology show Tales from the Darkside. Seasons of Belief was written and directed by Michael McDowell and is one of the highlights of season three. It's a traditional Christmas scene in a family home. Mum and Dad (played by Margaret Klenck and EG Marshall respectively) are sitting in their armchairs as the kids Jimbo (Sky Berdahl) and Stefa (Jenna von Oÿ) sprawl around on the floor with their crayons (and general impatience) as they wait for Christmas Day to arrive. There is a log fire crackling away and presents and decorations everywhere. How very nice.

The kids are easily bored and fidgety so the parents decide to tell them a Christmas story. This is a very weird Christmas story though and all about the Grither - a monster who lives in a cave at the North Pole. If you don't believe in the Grither he'll apparently come and visit you in person. Nonsense of course. Or is it?

Seasons of Belief is a great little episode. Not only do we get a nice Christmas atmosphere but also the great EG Marshall (surely one of the best actors to ever appear in Tales from the Darkside) telling a very strange spooky Christmas story for much of the episode. My only criticism would be that he looks too old to be married to Margaret Klenck and father to two small children but, anyway, let's not split hairs. They got EG Marshall and that was a minor coup.

This episode builds to a wonderful last act where, against all odds, it appears that the Grither might just be paying this family a most unexpected visit. What is great about Seasons of Belief is the way that it establishes this cosy family Christmas scene where we don't think anything bad can possibly happen but then twists this on its head and turns into a horror yarn at the end. This story becomes quite tense and scary at the end and, as Christmas and horror stories always go together wonderfully well, Seasons of Belief is very enjoyable.

The Grither is more implied than actually seen but the what practical effects we do get are a lot of fun and it's very entertaining when this family house comes under siege from this mythical monster. There is really not much to dislike about this episode at all. You've got EG Marshall, a wonderful Christmas atmosphere, and a fun story. This episode is quite magical in its best moments and then turns into a good monster/horror yarn. This is one of those Darkside episodes that you always find yourself watching again if you chance upon it on television and, of course, is a wonderful episode to watch at Christmas too.

Seasons of Belief is a really good episode with much to enjoy and - happily - one of those Darkside stories that gets better and better as it plays out. This would certainly rank as one of the most memorable episodes of (the sometimes up and down) season three. You could reasonably argue that Seasons of

Belief is worthy of a place at the hallowed Tales from the Darkside top table made up of the best stories from any season.

THE SHINING (1980)

Is Kubrick's famous adaption of Stephen King's novel The Shining a Christmas movie? Well, I'd say yes. It has snow, takes place in the dead of winter, and little Danny even seems to be wearing a Christmas pullover! Is there anyone alive who doesn't know what The Shining is about by now? Former teacher and recovering alcoholic Jack Torrance (Jack Nicholson) takes his wife Wendy (Shelley Duvall) and son Danny (Danny Lloyd) to the lonely and remote Overlook Hotel in the Colorado Rockies to take up a position as the winter caretaker.

It seems like the perfect place for budding writer Jack to get some work done and earn a little money in the process. Isolated, quiet, solitude, devoid of people. On arrival the manager warns Jack that a previous caretaker named Charles Grady was driven insane by the cabin fever of the Overlook in the winter and murdered his wife and twin daughters with an axe. Jack is not terribly worried about this (he jokes about how his wife will lap this story up because she's a horror junky) and the family do their best to settle in and get their bearings. But Jack's son Danny has a psychic gift that enables him to see the past and the future. The hotel chef Dick Hallorann (Scatman Crothers) - about to leave for his Winter holiday in Florida - recognises the ability in Danny because he has it too.

"I can remember when I was a little boy. My grandmother and I could hold conversations entirely without ever opening our mouths. She called it "shining". And for a long time, I thought it was just the two of us that had the shine to us. Just like you probably thought you was the only one. But there are other folks, though mostly they don't know it, or don't believe it.

Well, you know, when something happens, it can leave a trace of itself behind. Say like, if someone burns toast. Well, maybe things that happen leave other kinds of traces behind. Not things that anyone can notice, but things that people who "shine" can see. Just like they can see things that haven't happened yet. Well, sometimes they can see things that happened a long time ago. I think a lot of things happened right here in this particular hotel over the years... and not all of 'em was good."

Danny begins to see disturbing flashes of the past relating to the murders and is warned to stay away from a particular room. More troubling though is the mental deterioration of Jack. Suffering from severe writer's block and losing his grip on sanity in the alienating environment, he begins to see hallucinations/ghosts. One in particular, a butler named Delbert Grady (Phillip Stone) - presumably (and slightly confusingly) a manifestation of Charles Grady - tells Jack that he must "correct" his wife and son. Needless to say, wife and son are soon in very big trouble indeed.

The Shining is incredibly rich in atmosphere and a foreboding sense of dread and Kubrick does a fantastic job in designing and creating the hotel. The exteriors at the beginning of the film (pilfered for the original ending to Blade Runner) were shot in Colorado - the wonderful opening image of the Torrance car winding its way around the mountain roads from high above. Exteriors were shot at Elstree in Britain and great care is taken to make the hotel as strange and labyrinth as possible. A place where you really could lose your mind if you were not careful. The outdoor maze and the maze puzzle like hexagonal patterns on the carpets that stretch across the endless hallways of the Overlook. I suppose most people will remember Danny riding his little bike around these halls (inventive use of steadicam throughout The Shining) and meeting the murdered twins in a flashback. Some very creepy images in the film that stay with you.

It is for the most part a psychological horror rather than

Michael Myers stalking and slashing although it does seem to become more conventional in the final act. Lot of red again in this hotel by the way. One problem I do have with the film is that Jake Torrance goes bonkers so quickly its hard to even remember what he was like at the start of the film or if he was any different. Stephen King actually complained that Nicholson seemed mad from the off! The film seems more obsessed with writer's block than the alcoholism of the character. It seems to be this that has driven him mad as much as anything. Are there really ghosts in the hotel or is it all in his frazzled imagination? There seems to be a definite moment in the film where a supernatural explanation is the only conclusion but it would just about work the other way too.

There is probably not enough of Phillip Stone in this film and also good value is Joe Turkel as Lloyd the bartender, another ghost/hallucination who Jake meets and converses in a swanky period bar from the past. What about Jack Nicholson? This is arguably his most well known role but does it mark the slide from serious actor to someone who just turns up and does a nutty mad eyed Jack Nicholson turn? It maybe does. Nicholson is completely over the top here and for the first time becomes a caricature of himself.

There is some sense of nuance in earlier portions of the film but Nicholson goes mad so quickly that one's memory of The Shining is the film where where he does his mad scenery chewing Jack Nicholson turn rather than give a measured performance. I think he was better in One Flew Over the Cuckoos' Nest and some of his earlier films. You can't imagine anyone else playing Randle McMurphy but you could take a leap of imagination sort of imagine someone else playing Jake Torrance if Nicholson hadn't done it. James Woods or someone.

Nicholson does though give the film its iconic status. That blank scary look and the relish with which he delivers the films most notable (and blackly comic) one liners when his character goes doolally. The Overlook is rife with Native

American imagery and this seems to form a subtext about genocide and racism. I like the fact that Kubrick films leave you with more questions than answers. There is much that is open to interpretation here right down to the final image. Mention must go to Scatman Crothers too (what a great voice!). He's not in the film much but I love the scene where he shows Danny the food stores.

SILENT NIGHT, DEADLY NIGHT (1984)

Well, I suppose this one HAS to go in this book somewhere. Silent Night, Deadly Night is a 1984 horror film about a kid named Billy whose parents are murdered on Christmas Eve by a lunatic criminal dressed as Santa. After enduring life in a tough orphanage run by nuns, Billy grows up and is given a job as a stock boy in a toy store. Billy seems a decent young man but there is only problem. Any mention of Christmas or Santa gives him unwelcome flashbacks. When he is asked to dress up as Santa in the store for Christmas this tilts Billy over the edge and he goes on a murderous spree - all while dressed in a Santa suit.

This film was highly controversial on its release and didn't even get released in some countries. This controversy came as a complete surprise to the producers because everyone acted as if this was the first film to conflate Christmas (specifically Santa) with horror in this fashion. As they rightly noted though movies like Christmas Evil and Tales from the Crypt had already done this. It's hard these days to see what all the fuss was about. Silent Night, Deadly Night is far too silly a film to have provoked such protest.

Silent Night, Deadly Night is a bit rough around the edges with some wooden acting and cheesy musical montages and it takes an awfully long time to get to the Santa carnage but there are some decent enough death scenes when Billy turns murderous with his trusty axe. As far as eighties slashers go, this film is actually quite tame compared to a lot of them but should have just enough mayhem to please fans of low-budget eighties horror. Most of the film takes place in the toy store but the opening scenes, where Billy's doomed parents go to visit a nutty relative, are quite atmospheric.

Silent Night, Deadly Night is not John carpenter's Halloween but it is just about worth a look for horror completists who enjoy Christmas themed movies. This film became mildly cultish in the end and was turned into a franchise. Believe it or not, the fifth film in the franchise actually featured Mickey Rooney! You've probably got no good reason to watch all of these films but the first one is certainly watchable and sort of fun in a cheesy dated sort of way. If you've ever wanted to see someone impaled on reindeer antlers or decapitated while on a sled then Silent Night, Deadly Night is the movie for you.

SILENT NIGHT, DEADLY NIGHT PART 2 (1987)

Yes, this is one of the worst films ever made but it's so funny it simply has to go on our list. Silent Night, Deadly Night Part 2 is a 1987 horror sequel to 1984's Silent Night, Deadly Night. The first film featured a maniac who goes on a killing spree dressed as Santa Claus. It became highly controversial (which seems hard to believe these days) and gained a certain notoriety as a result. This 1987 sequel revolves around Ricky (Eric Freeman), the brother of the maniac from the first film. Ricky goes on his own killing spree and more carnage ensues.

This sequel was directed by an editor named Harry Lee. Apparently, he was asked to simply cut and mix the footage from the first film to create the illusion of a sequel but he insisted on being allowed to shoot something new.

Nonetheless, an awful lot of footage from the first film is shown to us again so if you have seen the original Silent Night, Deadly Night you might well feel a bit cheated.

Silent Night, Deadly Night Part 2 is one of those films that is so bad it has become something of a cultish comedy staple on YouTube. Much of this is thanks to the atrocious acting of Eric Freeman as our murderous main character. Freeman's line readings are very amusing at times. "Garbage day!" Freeman is truly one of the worst actors in history - so much so that he's hilarious in this film.

The actual film (what there is of it away from the flashbacks) is rather cheesy and silly compared to the first film. Silent Night, Deadly Night was not Ingmar Bergman but it did feel more competent and atmospheric than this sequel. Silent Night, Deadly Night Part 2 is good for a laugh though and as such is hard to resist.

THE SNOWMAN (1982)

The Snowman is a 1982 animated film based on the graphic novel of the same name by the great Raymond Briggs. This film is a beloved Christmas staple in Britain. In the story, a boy wakes up one morning and is excited to find a thick blanket of snow has fallen outside. He decides to build a snowman and later that night the snowman magically comes to life and is invited indoors by the boy. Various capers ensue, with a late night feast, exploration of the house, and flying through the night sky ...

According to Raymond Briggs, it was his previous book, the brilliant Fungus the Bogeyman, that inspired The Snowman. Fungus the Bogeyman was wordy, dense and dark and after spending a couple of years mired in the slime drenched existential subterranean world of Fungus, Briggs wanted to do something clean and more pleasant and make it much simpler, wordless in fact. The Snowman is therefore very different from Fungus the Bogeyman but just as effective in what it sets out to do.

Apparently, the idea of a snowman coming to life was something he'd come up with several years before (I sometimes wonder though if Briggs ever read 'Silent Snow, Secret Snow', a cult 1934 short story by Conrad Aiken about a boy who can't face reality and constantly daydreams about snow). After completing Fungus the Bogeyman it seemed like the perfect time for his snowman idea. There is something very cosy and comforting about the art in the work of Raymond Briggs and this is certainly true of The Snowman with its wintry atmosphere of snow, scarves, candles, and houses with welcoming lights glowing dimly from inside.

There are a few differences between this film and the book that should probably be mentioned. Unlike the film, the book is not set during Christmas but merely during the winter. I don't think the somewhat morose Raymond Briggs was the world's biggest fan of Christmas to be honest! The section in the film where the little boy and the snowman visit the North Pole and see Father Christmas is not in the book at all but an extra addition by the makers of the film. I gather Raymond Briggs rolled his eyes at all of this but I personally like both the Christmassy trappings of the film and the slightly more restrained and slightly less sentimental Raymond Briggs nature of the original book.

There is, famously, a poignant and sad quality to the film and it's slightly more pronounced in the book with a subtext about the loss of innocence and the fleeting nature of things. Briggs had recently lost both his parents and his wife when he worked on the book in the seventies and some of the feelings and thoughts he had at time found their way into the story. One other difference too I find is that the friendship between the boy and the snowman is much more dreamlike in the book.

It is open to question in the book whether or not the snowman was real or merely a fantasy or dream. The film is not quite so ambiguous and makes a small but significant change to the ending. Briggs felt that the wordlessness here was perfect for the wintry setting as snow conveys an aura of serenity and silence. The house in the story is based on his own house on the South Downs. The Snowman manages to convey depth and feelings and the bittersweet fleeting, unlikely and intense friendship in the book (a common feature of Briggs's work) remains touching and imaginative. This is still a lovely film to watch. It's a mug of cocoa on a frosty day and remains an enduring children's classic.

STAR TREK: GENERATIONS (1994)

Yes, this film has a Christmas scene so it offers me a perfect excuse to shoehorn Star Trek into this book! Star Trek: Generations was released in 1994 and written by Ronald D Moore and Brannon Braga. The original story was conceived by the much maligned Star Trek television producer Rick Berman. One immediate problem is that the film was directed David Carson, a man who had directed several episodes of the television series but had no experience with feature films. He's competent and parts of the film look good but the pacing is sometimes off and the action sequences (not that there are many of them) are mostly by the numbers and lack pizzazz.

The plan by Paramount had been for Leonard Nimoy to direct the film and take on an acting role as Spock alongside the rest of the original cast in a symbolic passing of the torch to the Next Generation crew. Nimoy though didn't think much of Berman's premise and decided he wanted no part of the film either behind the camera or in front of it. DeForest Kelley also declined to make an appearance as Dr McCoy and so in the end you only get Captain Kirk (William Shatner of course), Scotty (James Doohan) and Chekov (Walter Koenig) in a sort of prologue.

The title sequence is quite clever and reasonably arresting. A champagne bottle seems to spin endlessly through the eternity of space during the credits and eventually smashes against a metallic white hull revealed to be the Enterprise-B on its maiden journey out of space dock in the year 2293. Kirk, Scotty and Chekov are onboard as honoured guests with a gaggle of excited press. All are feeling their age as they survey the young crew. Captain Harriman (Alan Ruck of Ferris Bueller's Day Off fame) is in charge of the Enterprise now but we soon learn he's no Captain Kirk when an unexpected crisis develops.

The celebration jaunt out of space dock for the new Enterprise turns into a rescue mission when a distress call is detected from two refugee packed ships caught up in a strange swirling energy ribbon. Harriman turns out to be an indecisive wuss and hands the command of the ship over to Kirk in the panic. Kirk immediately goes to sit in the Captain's chair and then thinks better of it (quite a good moment this). It's not his ship anymore and Harriman must take responsibility now. Anyway, Kirk goes below to do something with the deflector shields (pseudo science techno waffle device for plot purposes) and saves fifty refugees but the energy ribbon tears out the section of the ship he was working in, leaving only a gaping hole and force fields that reveal the vast blackness of space when Scotty and Chekov go down to check on him.

Kirk is presumed dead and the film then moves on several decades to the year 2371 where Captain Picard is now in charge of the USS Enterprise-D with a crew that wall be very familiar indeed to anyone who watched the Next Generation television series. Picard receives a distress call from a solar observatory where they discover that everyone has been killed save for scientist named Doctor Tolian Soran (Malcolm McDowell).

Enterprise bartender and mystic know it all Guinan (Whoopi

Goldberg) tells Picard and she and Soren were both rescued by the Enterprise-B all those years ago. Her (alien) race lives a very long time but Soren's secret to such a long life is the mysterious energy ribbon. It is a Nexus where "time has no meaning" and one enters a state of permanent bliss - like being inside a dream forever. Soran has one chance to get back inside the Nexus and is altering the path of the energy ribbon by collapsing stars. Millions of people on the planet Veridian III will die if Soren is successful and it's up to Picard to stop him.

The most frequent criticism of the Next Generation films is that they often feel like two back to back episodes of the television rather than a grand big screen cinematic adventure and Star Trek: Generations is certainly guilty of this at times. Some special effects shots of the Enterprise from the television series are actually reused (I believe the film only went into production ten days after the television series ended) and this seems a bit cheapjack and mean when it happens.

The crew disappointingly have the same uniforms and sets that inhabited the small screen incarnation too. New costumes were designed but slung out at the last minute after someone (presumably) decided they were rubbish. Uniforms from the then still running Star Trek television series Deep Space Nine were hastily borrowed and if you look at Jonathan Frakes in particular you'll see that his uniform is clearly way too small for him!

The best sequences in the film are the introduction of the Next Generation crew in a holodeck programme where Worf is receiving a nautical themed promotion on a sailing ship (I believe it was shot on the Lady Washington) in the high seas and a much later set-piece that has the Enterprise having to split into two different parts before the saucer section crash lands on a planet. The first scene gives the film a bit of scope and is fun while the latter is the grand set-piece and gives you the biggest bang for your money. It goes on a bit but it's well staged and the most cinematic flourish in the film, throwing far more mayhem at the screen than the television series could.

Generations seems to take its cue from The Wrath of Khan with the major theme time and mortality. Picard learns at the start of the film that his young nephew has died in a fire. He's distraught and filled with sadness at the thought of a life that ended before it really started and also reflecting on getting older and wondering what his legacy will be. "Captain. Aren't you beginning to feel time gaining on you?" says Soren. "It's like a predator. It's stalking you. Oh, you can try and outrun it with doctors, medicines, new technologies, but in the end, time is going to hunt you down and make the kill."

Stewart plays this well early on, especially when Soren tells him this. Picard's brusque confident aura is suddenly broken for a moment and he seems vulnerable. The film is of course most notable for Picard and Captain Kirk meeting at last when Picard enters the nexus and finds Kirk there - or at least an echo of Kirk. In the Nexus Picard finds he has a wife and adoring children. There is a roaring fire and presents scattered around a big lavish house. Very Charles Dickens.

Actually, the meeting of the two Captains is rather anti-climatic in the end. Shatner seems to be enjoying himself and has a few good lines ("I don't need to be lectured by you. I was out saving the galaxy when your grandfather was in diapers!") but they just end up fighting Soren on a bridge in the desert. I really feel they should have either had the whole original series crew as part of the film in a more substantial way or just left Picard and his friends to it. Shatner feels like a contrived guest star and I don't care much for how they leave the character of Kirk here.

Stewart and Shatner have practically no chemistry at all (which is unsurprising I suppose as they were from different shows) and they seem somewhat incongruous acting together here. Shatner has a twinkle in his eye and is over egging his part while Stewart is taking everything very seriously!

Malcolm McDowell is remarkably restrained all things considering and chews far less scenery than Ricardo Montalban and Christopher Lloyd did as previous Star Trek baddies. You get a sense that he's rather bored and just paying the bills and consequently Soren doesn't emerge as an especially memorable villain.

As usual in this series, it's Brent Spiner as Data who is the mot notable presence after Stewart. Data has an emotion chip fitted here (you have to be familiar with the television series to fully get this development) so he can be more human. So gets scared, laughs etc, and while this is mildly interesting to a point it soon becomes annoying and makes you wish he'd turn it off and go back to be being the emotionless always getting the wrong end of the stick Data we are used to. It does provide perhaps the most amusing moment in the film though when Data swears during a tense moment for the Enterprise.

Some of the exposition that is offered as an olive branch for more general audiences is a trifle annoying at times. For example, at the start of the film Data explains that he doesn't understand the concept of humour. If you've watched about 600 episodes of Star Trek: The Next Generation then you really don't need to be told that Data doesn't understand humour. We know. He's an android without emotions!

This is a surprisingly talky film for much of its running time and a space battle involving some Klingons (when it does arrive) seems flat and uninspired, as do the phaser shoots out on the observatory. The film often looks drab and too much like a television series and so the scenes of Picard and Soren on the rocky desert planet Veridian III are actually welcome from a visual point of view at least as they add some colour and scope to the film with the location shooting in Nevada. Star Trek: Generations is watchable though and certainly not a terrible film. it could have been better but it's certainly not a clunker by any means.

STRANGER THINGS (SEASON ONE) - 2016

Ok, it might be stretching (ahem) things to call the first season of stranger things a Christmas show but it takes place in winter, Christmas lights are an important part of the story, there is snow, and a Christmas epilogue complete with carols. That's good enough for me! This is a great show and season one will always be my favourite.

The premise of Stranger Things is relatively simple on the surface despite the scientific trappings and numerous pop culture Easter eggs. Dredging up inspiration from many novels, stories, movies, tv shows, and video games, the show concerns a group of characters in a small (and fictional) Indiana town named Hawkins. The local Department of Energy - in the form of the Hawkins Lab - has opened a dimensional rift (rather like in Stephen King's The Mist) which is a portal to a hostile and nightmare version of our own world. A faceless monster (which the boys in the show dub the Demogorgon because of their love of Dungeons & Dragons) begins to move to and thro from this world and ours.

A little boy named Will Byers is pulled into the other dimension (dubbed the Upside Down by the kids) and so a search for him begins with police chief Hopper, his mother Joyce Byers, and his friends all conducting their own investigations. Into this mix we throw Eleven, a little girl with telekinetic powers who escaped from the Hawkins Lab. She is secretly sheltered by Will's friends and might be the key to finding him. A teenager named Barb is also snared by the monster and her friend Nancy also becomes embroiled in seeking to get to the bottom of the strange events happening around the fringes of this small town.

Despite the many influences of Stranger Things (which the show doesn't shy away from), it still feels unique enough to stand on its own feet. There is genuine horror, action, and plenty of wit from both the cast and the scripts. The show is beautifully designed and has a memorable synth score by Survive. At its best, Stranger Things is about as much fun as a tv show can get and each new season is eagerly anticipated (and rapidly binged when it arrives).

Season one of Stranger Things is a perfectly contained story that would work fine as a limited miniseries. There would be more Stranger Things of course, but taken as one story, this is a perfectly paced and compelling tale with lashings of heart and some good laughs. While you would not exactly say the material was original, it works in the context of a show that is affectionate and open about its influences. Stranger Things is beautifully produced and has a wonderful music score. The ace up its sleeve though is the cast and the memorable characters they essay.

What is most admirable is the way that the characters in Stranger Things have their own arcs and quests. They all develop. Take Hopper for example. He's world weary and slobbish when we first meet him but the search for Will brings forth all the qualities that he had hidden deep inside. Dedication, bravery, selflessness, kindness. Nancy goes from vacuous teen to warrior. Steve goes from absolute douche to hero (he even seems to have won Nancy back as this finale draws to its end). Eleven goes from victim to protector. And so on. Stranger Things, produced with such little publicity as it was, was a pleasant surprise when it arrived in 2016 and deserved the huge acclaim and fandom it generated.

TALES FROM THE CRYPT (1972)

Tales from the Crypt is the best known of the Amicus anthology films and was based on the infamous and influential (everyone from Stephen King to George Romero grew up loving them) 1950s EC horror and suspense comics published by William Gaines. The enjoyably lurid and colourful comics (which were rather gruesome and risque - although tongue-in-cheek and with their own twisted sense of karma and morality) offered all manner of deaths, monsters, zombies, murders, ghosts, and general macabre mayhem stirred by greed, lust and envy until parents began to notice what their children were reading and the comics were banned - even becoming the subject of Congressional subcommittee hearings.

The film opens with shots around an old graveyard and Bach's Toccata and Fugue in D minor. It's an Amicus Production, it's the seventies, and you know you are in for some kitsch retro fun. As usual, we get several different short horror tales all linked together by a framing device, in this case it's five strangers visiting some labyrinthine underground catacombs. They become a bit lost and end up in a strange 'skull' room where the door shuts behind them. The monkish Crypt Keeper appears, played by none other than Ralph Richardson, and, in an old thesp in a seventies horror film sort of way, begins to talk about their future and respective fates...

And All Through The House'is the first story and features good old Joan Collins as Joanne Clayton. Joan was having a career crisis around this time but the home grown horror industry was on hand and would soon lead to her being involved in a love triangle with a tree and Michael Jayston in Tales That Witness Madness. But first this... it's Christmas Eve and carol singers sing sweetly from a very seventies radio as the camera pans around an equally seventies piece of interior decor. Joanne's husband settles down with a newspaper to enjoy this lovely moment of seasonal calm and anticipation... before blood splatters over his paper and we cut to Joanne/Joan looking very pleased with herself and holding some sort of sword. Yes, she's done away with him for the insurance but can she cover her tracks and make it look like an accident? And what was that local newsflash on the radio? A homicidal maniac has just escaped? Dressed as Father Christmas? You'd better make sure all of those windows and doors are locked...

And All Through The House is fun start to the film and Joan Collins is good value as usual. Joan spends much of this segment alone with no dialogue but is always watchable. She has some wonderful panto facial expressions at various points and must have one of the finest smirks of all time. It's also a reasonably gripping tale as Joanne attempts to dispose of the blood and body etc. The Christmas atmosphere adds to the creepiness of the segment (even the carols sound strangely eerie) and they make good use of snow, rattly windows and sound effects in his one. There is one really good moment that will make you jump too. This piece does a pretty good job of maintaining some suspense over its short running time and although it doesn't have a tremendously surprising ending it is a fun opening story for the anthology.

Reflection Of Death features Ian Hendry as Carl Maitland and is an adequate enough second portion of compendium capers. We see Carl emotionally saying goodbye to his children as they snooze away in their bunk beds at the start of this segment. Carl, the bounder, is walking out on them and his wife to be with young bit on the side Susan (played by Angela Grant). They drive away down the motorway at night but are involved in a crash that spins the car over several times. Carl wakes up and staggers away from the wreckage to find help. The problem is, every person he meets or tries to flag down just screams at the mere sight of him. What has happened to Carl?

This is less campy than some of the other segments but fairly gripping. It looks really good in places, especially in the aftermath of the car smash with flames and a blurry light. They shoot everything from Carl's perspective so the reactions of everyone to him are a bit scarier and more intriguing, making it all a trifle creepier. There is a 'revelation' shot that will make you jump a little if you've never seen it before and overall it's quite a tight and interesting story. The ending is a bit of a cop out though and, like several other characters in these films, you do wonder what exactly was so terrible about

Carl's behaviour for him to end up in front of the Crypt Keeper. He didn't kill anyone, he just left his wife!

Poetic Justice features the great Peter Cushing, here giving a very endearing and sweet performance as a kind old widower called Arthur Grymsdyke who makes toys for the local children and looks after a huge collection of cats and dogs that help alleviate his loneliness. Arthur's ramshackle house though is situated in an increasingly upmarket neighbourhood and snobby posh git James (Robin Phillips) from across the road finds himself more and more irritated by having this eccentric and slightly disorganised old man living near him and ruining the view. He begins a campaign to remove him and becomes more and more cold-hearted in his obsessive quest to drive Grymsdyke out...

Poetic Justice is a really good segment. Peter Cushing is wonderful as usual and always very watchable. His incredibly sympathetic performance is a major plus here. It has been speculated that Cushing's character echoed his own life and grief for his late wife and he certainly pulls on the heartstrings. There is a bit that is almost too sad to watch when he reads out horrible Valentines cards sent to him. Robin Phillips is excellent also as the scheming villain of the piece, plotting the removal of Grymsdyke from his large study. The grisly ending is very satisfying in this one and great fun. This segment does come the closest I feel to evoking the spirit of EC Comics.

Wish You Were Here is a variation on 'The Monkey's Paw' and not bad. Richard Greene plays a businessman called Ralph Jason who is struggling to keep his finances above water. Barbara Murray, as his wife, finds a Chinese antique and wishes for a fortune to help them out. This has rather unfortunate consequences for her husband to say the least...

A decent enough, though weird segment, with quite a shocking conclusion. It has a good creepy atmosphere throughout although it is slightly inconsistent in tone, with a bit where some pallbearers are carrying a coffin into a house coming across like something out of an Eric Sykes skit. This story doesn't actually make an awful lot of sense when you think about it afterwards but to analyse films like this too much is probably to miss the point - and fun. One fun element to this one is seeing 'Death' following Greene on a motorcycle, quite literally, as they race through the countryside of Amicus Land!

The best is - in my opinion - saved for last with Blind Alleys. "In the kingdom of the blind the one-eyed man is King," says Major William Rogers, wonderfully played by Nigel Patrick. The Major has taken over as the new boss of Elmridge Home For The Blind, an anachronistic, ramshackle institution that is apparently always surrounded by snow and a howling wind. Rogers immediately begins a new cost cutting operation which involves a reduction on the heating and food for the residents. But the Major is making no such concessions in his own office - which he is even buying new paintings for!

The scene where Patrick is seen tucking into a huge lunch beside a roaring fire in his office after the frozen blind folk have been fobbed off with watery soup in the canteen is probably one of the funniest in cinema history. "Why don't you all go to bed?" says the incredibly tactful and sensitive Major when they complain about the lack of heating. "You can't see anything anyway." The residents of Elmridge are soon plotting what becomes a somewhat implausible but enjoyable revenge...

Tales From The Crypt is campy, very British fun with one or two twists and turns and a couple of good shocks. Freddie Francis always manages to make to film look interesting with bright garish colours in some scenes and an eerie fog in others and the cast is good fun, taking in everyone from Joan Collins to Patrick Magee. I have a great deal of affection for the Amicus anthology films and Tales From The Crypt is right up there with the best of them.

TANGERINE (2015)

Tangerine is a low budget comedy drama about two transgender sex workers named Sin-Dee Rella and Alexandra (played by Kitana Kiki Rodriguez and Mya Taylor respectively) and their various misadventures on Christmas Eve as Sin-Dee Rella attempts to find her boyfriend after hearing stories that he's been cheating on her. A series of vignettes follows as our our two main characters hit the streets of Loas Angeles.

The most remarkable thing about this film is that it was shot entirely using iPhones so has a street level rough and ready sort of feel which works surprisingly well. The film takes us down into the underbelly of Los Angeles and has an authenticity which mainstream Hollywood films obviously tend to lack. You really believe in the characters in Tangerine and the performances are full of energy. This is a film that has many downbeat elements but it is also funny too with the lead characters zipping out an array of crude sarcastic retorts.

It probably goes without saying that this film will not be for all tastes and it does have what you might describe as some adults only content but it is a likeable film and also - crucially - a Christmas film too, though not what you would call a traditional Christmas film. If you like indie films and Christmas films which offer something different then Tangerine is certainly worth a look. It's one of those films which is hard to describe and better just experienced. If you fall for the rough and ready charms of the film then you should find this a rewarding and engaging experience.

TOKYO GODFATHERS (2003)

Tokyo Godfathers is a Japanese animated film directed by Satoshi Kon. The film was inspired by John Ford's 3 Godfathers. The premise has three homeless people – a middle-aged alcoholic man named Gin, a transgender woman named Hana, and a dependent teenage runaway girl named Miyuki – finding an abandoned baby and trying to return the baby to its parents. The story takes place on Christmas Eve.

Even those who don't usually watch Japanese anime might themselves charmed by Tokyo Godfathers - which is surely one of the best Christmas animated films ever made. The film has plenty of Christmas atmosphere and is about family, coincidence, and life on the margins of society. This film is quite fast paced and has memorable characters. There are plenty of twists and turns too so the film is never too predictable.

The animation takes a bit of getting used to at first but you'll soon settle into it and get caught up in the sweep of the story and the rich festive aura which pervades the piece. This is not a cartoon that kids can watch and is rather dark but ultimately it is a strangely uplifting story about miracles, coincidence, and the ties that bind people - even if they don't actually know one another. Tokyo Godfathers is regarded to be something of a masterpiece by animation fans and was highly lauded by critics when it was released back in 2003.

TRADING PLACES (1983)

Trading Places in a 1983 John Landis comedy film which has a fairly high reputation and plenty of funny scenes. Is this a Christmas film? Well, yes I suppose. There is snow, Dan Akroyd dresses up as Santa, and there even a Christmas party sequence! The plot concerns wealthy Randolph and Mortimer Duke (played by Ralph Bellamy and Don Ameche), two wealthy brothers who run a commodities brokerage firm.

In order to amuse themselves, these heartless businessmen come up with a nature vs nurture bet. They take the successful Louis Winthorpe III (Dan Aykroyd), their managing director, and completely wreck his life - to the point where he becomes a suicidal homeless bum. They replace him with a homeless street hustler named Billy Ray Valentine (Eddie Murphy). However, Winthorpe and Valentine eventually learn that they've been manipulated purely for a bet and plot their revenge.

Trading Places is for the most part a lot of fun. It supplies an early role for Eddie Murphy and he's full of energy and comic charisma here in his eighties heyday. Aykroyd is also terrific as Winthorpe. This movie was actually conceived as vehicle for Gene Wilder and Richard Pryor and while you can easily imagine those two playing these roles, Murphy and Akroyd certainly make a good team. The scenes where Winthorpe hits rock bottom in particular are very funny in a darkly comic fashion.

There's a great cast in this film too with Jamie Lee Curtis as a prostitute who helps Winthorpe and Denholm Elliott as his butler. The film is definitely at its best when these two very different men find themselves being 'switched' and assuming the position of one another in life and only really sags a bit near the end when we have some nonsense with a gorilla and then the elaborate financial revenge plot (which is not as much fun as the earlier stuff in the movie) but these are minor quibbles really. If you want a few laughs with a Christmas theme then Trading Places will certainly deliver that.

THE 12 DAYS OF CHRISTINE (2015)

The 12 Days of Christine is a 2015 episode of the excellent anthology series Inside No.9. The 12 Days of Christine has some obvious allusions to A Christmas Carol - although the two stories are very different. The concept of someone experiencing confusing 'time jumps' is familiar in film and television fantasy but The 12 Days of Christine is rather unique in the way that this concept is used to present a bittersweet drama. The 12 Days of Christine is about the nature of memories and this theme is used for some misdirection in the episode. Many people thought they had worked out what was happening to Christine but then had their expectations subverted by the ending.

In this episode a young woman named Christine (Sheridan Smith) arrives home from a New Year's Eve party with Adam (Tom Riley). Suddenly, thirteen months have passed. We see Christine get married, pregnant, divorced, and become confused by the way that her life seems to be jumbled together into a series of events that don't have a conventional chronological structure. Christine seems to be jumping from point to point through time and has no idea why. And who exactly is the mysterious unknown man she keeps having visions of?

The 12 Days of Christine is a rather difficult episode to describe or place into any particular category. The only thing to really say is that this is uniquely Inside No. 9 and in all probability the best episode this show has ever produced or ever will produce. The 12 Days of Christine is just about the most perfect half an hour of television you are ever likely to watch.

What starts as a domestic drama about an ordinary young woman and her ups and downs in life quickly becomes a most compelling mystery when Christine begins to shuttle through time - her journey charted by twelve years and notable times or events. We see her at New Year's Eve, Christmas, Halloween, Bonfire Night, her 30th birthday, and so on. But the time between these events seems to have vanished. Christine seems to be plucking out events and fragments of life and then experiencing them in isolation. Her circumstances change in each experience, as do the people around her - marking the passage of time.

The 12 Days of Christine is not what you would describe as one of the more comic episodes of Inside No. 9 but it does have plenty of wit and humour scattered throughout its running time. Some of the early scenes are vaguely reminiscent of The Royle Family but it soon becomes a compelling drama with some surreal horror flourishes. This blending of different genres is done so brilliantly that we never experience any jarring shifts in tone.

Throughout the story we become increasingly fascinated by the plight of Christine and - like the character herself - are desperate to understand the source of the mystery she seems to find herself in. Christine seems to be losing memories and time. She experiences some memorable occasions but where has all the time in between gone?

Sheridan Smith, who gives a remarkable performance in The 12 Days of Christine, is perfectly at home in comedy and so makes the most of what funny lines Shearsmith and Pemberton do supply. Her acting chops are also more than a match for the drama that comes her way too. She makes Christine a very believable, human, and likeable character. The construction of a set for this episode to depict Christine's flat reaps some rich rewards because it gives everything an air of complete authenticity. We really do come to believe in the world of this character as a real and realistic place. The tension between this mundane realistic backdrop and the strange experiences and visions of Christine supplies the mystery and drama.

Christine's domestic trials feel convincing too. We see the excitement of marriage and parenthood but then - over time - it becomes apparent that Adam in particular is growing tired of this and feeling suffocated by his responsibilities. This leaves poor Christine alone with the responsibilities (although she does of course have help from her loyal mother). This all makes Christine a likeable and relatable sort of character. Life isn't perfect but she's doing her best - a situation that most people can identify with.

The structure of The 12 Days of Christine led many viewers to suspect that they were watching a story about memory loss. They wondered if Christine was suffering from some sort of dementia and perhaps this was her thinking of the past - trying to dredge up fogged memories but starting to find gaps in her attempts to remember her life. That would clearly have been a powerful story and probably would have made sense as an explanation for her plight, but - ultimately - this wasn't the case. It is possible though that there was some degree of misdirection to this end.

Paul Copley gives a moving performance as Christine's Alzheimer's afflicted father Ernie (is Ernie the reason why many people assumed this story was going to be about Christine losing her memory?) and Michele Dotrice is terrific as Christine's mother. Pemberton is quite amusing in support as Bobby - Christine's gay friend and fellow worker at Clarks. I like Bobby's comment during Christmas dinner that they'll be "hearing" from the sprouts again soon! These characters are all played so well that you genuinely come to believe in them as real people.

Shearsmith plays a strange man who Christine seems to experience visions of in the story. In one scene she thinks he might be trying to steal her baby son. This character is a classic (and more obvious) piece of misdirection in a sense as it makes us anticipate a horror episode - or the very least some sort of horror denouement. The apparently supernatural and time travel elements are more or less red herrings in the grand scheme of things and that is part of what makes The 12 Days of Christine so brilliant.

The horror tinged scenes are very well staged and directed with power cuts and confusion over what is real or not. Shearsmith's character seems to be ghostly in that only Christine can see him. When we finally work out what is really happening it suddenly all makes perfect sense and we can't believe we didn't think of it sooner - for the clues were there all along. When Christine works out for herself what is happening and then accepts her fate, the ending is incredibly moving and powerful - especially with the use of Con te partirò, performed by Andrea Bocelli.

This is pretty much a flawless episode of Inside No. 9. The story is strange and compelling, the performances are fantastic, the episode is funny, creepy, and heartbreaking (all of these qualities blended perfectly by the script and the cast), and the highly emotional twist is one of the most memorable in the history of the show.

The 12 Days of Christine is a brilliant and moving drama and an episode that should be right at the top of the pile when it comes to compiling lists of the best entries in this show. This is an episode that manages to get everything right and produce 'lightning in a bottle' - especially when it comes to the poignant ending. Reece Shearsmith and Steve Pemberton must have been delighted when they saw what an amazing episode of Inside No. 9 their story had inspired.

WE'RE NO ANGELS (1955)

We're No Angels is a comic film which is set on Christmas Eve and Christmas Day. Three convicts – Joseph (Humphrey Bogart), Albert (Aldo Ray) and Jules (Peter Ustinov) – escape from prison on Devil's Island in French Guiana and make their way to a nearby town where they end up helping out at a struggling store after initially plan to rob the place and flee on a boat. The trio will have to make a decision though on what their true intentions will be.

We're No Angels is an agreeable comedy caper with plenty of Christmas spirit. It's a nice idea to have three crooks using their criminal skills to the advantage of a struggling business and the film is very well cast. Bogart in particular shows a nice talent for deadpan comedy here. Basil Rathbone turns up as the nominal 'baddie' and the fine cast makes this an engaging and amusing experience. The film is definitely a bit on the long side at over 100 minutes though and could definitely have been trimmed somewhat.

The constrictive nature of the film (it mostly plays out in a few store sets) is not a major hindrance and makes this rather like watching a comic play at times. We're No Angels is fun on the whole and worth a look if you've never seen it before. This film was remade in 1989 with Robert De Niro and Sean Penn and earned decidedly mixed reviews. You should definitely stick with the original. The original We're No Angels is just nice undemanding fun from Old Hollywood and a good film to watch during the festive period.

WHITE CHRISTMAS (1954)

Bing Crosby, Danny Kaye, Irving Berlin, I'm dreaming of a White Christmas etc. Well, you just knew this film was going to sneak into the list in the end didn't you? This is an obvious choice (TOO obvious maybe - and Clark Griswold in National Lampoon's Christmas Vacation would definitely agree with that!) but it is one of the most iconic and famous Christmas films of all time. White Christmas simply has to get a mention in any list of the greatest Christmas movies.

The film was directed Michael Curtiz and has Crosby and Kaye as two army buddies who form a showbusiness double-act after the war ends. They end up trying to save an inn run by their old army boss Major General Tom Waverly (Dean Jagger) in Pine Tree, Vermont over Christmas. There is no snow in Pine tree this Christmas but I'm pretty sure that state of affairs will change by the time the film ends! Along the way the duo hook up with Rosemary Clooney and Vera-Ellen and, well, I'm sure you probably know the rest by now.

This film will certainly be a trifle sentimental for some tastes but Danny Kaye is always fun and the colour and widescreen looks terrific. This is one of those films that nearly always seems to be playing in the background somewhere on Christmas morning and as such it probably wouldn't quite feel like Christmas if it wasn't there somewhere or other lurking on the fringes of your living room. White Christmas is far from my favourite Cristmas movie but for historical festive significance it simply has to go on this list.

THE YEAR WITHOUT SANTA CLAUS (1974)

This is another Rankin/Bass cartoon themed around Christmas. In the story Santa Claus (voiced by Mickey Rooney) is a bit fed-up up with Christmas and his task of delivering presents to a load of kids (who Santa's doctor says are probably ungrateful anyway!) and is consequently feeling under the weather. You could say that Santa here rather anticipates Raymond Briggs' Father Christmas in the fashion that he's a trifle grumpy about his job. Anyway, Mrs Claus (Shirley Booth) is rather alarmed that Santa has given up on Christmas so assigns two elves to go and talk to children to prove to Santa that he really is appreciated and much needed.

This is another very likeable stop-motion animation that isn't maybe quite as magical as some other Christmas cartoon classics but is still very enjoyable nonetheless. The cartoon is a bit on the chintzy side at times but has plenty of festive atmosphere and is actually quite funny in places. There are a few songs and a fine cast of voice actors - including Dick Shawn as the Snow Miser. I think this cartoon is rather on the long side at 50 minutes but it should keep kids happy on Christmas Day morning. You wouldn't say that The Year Without Santa Claus is an absolute classic but it is pretty good for what it is and the story and concept is rather endearing too.

YOUNG SHERLOCK HOLMES (1985)

This is a subtle Christmas film but it has snow, takes place just before Christmas, mentions Christmas Day in the coda, and generally has a festive atmosphere. So it goes on our list. Young Sherlock Holmes is a 1985 adventure film directed by Barry Levinson and written by Chris Columbus. This is film that veers into horror a surprising number of times. The story depicts a young Holmes (Nicholas Rowe) and Watson (Alan Cox) meeting at the exclusive Brompton Academy as schoolboys and shows us how they become friends and solve their first mystery together.

Holmes' embryonic deductive powers are put to the test when apparently healthy and normal men start suffering deadly hallucinations before dying in what appear to be suicides. When Mr Bobster (Patrick Newell) and Rev Nesbitt (Donald Eccles) fall victim, Holmes believes he has stumbled across a link to the deaths and attempts vainly to convince the police investigator, Lestrade (Roger Ashton-Griffiths). There is of course much more to the whole affair as Holmes discovers when he attempts to unravel this mystery with the help of Watson, nutty inventor and mentor Waxflatter (Nigel Stock) and his first great love Elizabeth (Sophie Ward).

Young Sherlock Holmes is an interesting, occasionally charming film that creates a rich and enjoyable Victorian atmosphere (naturally it always seems to be snowing) with numerous little references and jokes for the benefit of Conan Doyle fans. Unfortunately, the film loses its way at some stage and frequently bombards the viewer with far too much action and special effects work as it slips uncomfortably into Indiana Jones and the Temple of Doom territory. The end result is not completely without interest though for Sherlock Holmes fans and the lanky and floppy-haired Nicholas Rowe - who looks a lot like a youthful Oscar Wilde - is inspired casting as the young Holmes.

You do actually feel like Rowe could become the adult Sherlock Holmes we know so well when he grows older and we amusingly see how he picked up some of his more specific stereotypical traits and accessories - like his deerstalker hat and pipe. "On second thoughts, take it off! It looks very silly!" comments Watson when Holmes tries on his iconic headgear for the first time. Although the film plays fast and loose at times with the Holmes canon, it displays a palpable affection for Conan Doyle and the world he created, attempting with varying degrees of success to give it all a diverting twist.

One of the best things about the film is the warm and enjoyable narration throughout by Michael Hordern as the elderly Watson looking back on his first meeting with Holmes. Hordern's distinctive voice and nostalgic narration adds a good dose of charm and cosiness into a film that is often a bit too frantic and modern for its own good. "It was a cold, snowy day in early December," recalls Watson via the narration at the beginning of the film. "Lack of funds had forced my old school to close. I was being sent to a new one. I was in the heart of London at the height of the Victorian Era. The streets were teeming with every activity imaginable. I was very taken by what I saw. As I stepped from my carriage, the sight of my new school filled me with fear and apprehension, yet, I was swept with a wave of curiosity. However, nothing could prepare me for the extraordinary adventure that lay ahead, or the extraordinary individual who would change my life." It helps a great deal that Hordern's rich voice seems to belong to a bygone era.

The major weakness with Young Sherlock Holmes is that it does ultimately slip between two stools and give one a sense of two different films competing against one another. The Victorian atmosphere, Holmes in-jokes and references and detective elements would - I think - have sufficed alone to make an enjoyable and entertaining film speculating on Holmes as a schoolboy. There are though never quite enough of these elements to satisfy and the film gradually slides into increasingly tiresome chases and fights as it blitzes the viewer with special effects.

While the adventure elements are not without their charms and of course the young Holmes, an athletic and brave fellow and expert fencer, would have his scrapes and physical escapades in the course of an investigation, the action and effects often seem jarring and overplayed and sometimes rather too nasty for the young audience the film is intended for. Young Sherlock Holmes could I feel have been a lot more restrained and toned down all the stained glass windows coming to life, zombies, and Egyptian temple capers. I do though like the fact that the film looks like it cost a lot of money to make. A Spielbergian gloss is daubed all over Young Sherlock Holmes with snowy Victorian streets, horse drawn carriages and looming great rooms and set decorations.

Rowe presents us with a Holmes who not yet become detached from life and is still youthful and enthusiastic but there are nice little moments of sadness and reflection that point to the more complex person he will become as an adult. He has an air of arrogance and a sometimes terse quality that reminds you of the literary Holmes but obviously this is a rather watered down, family friendly version of Holmes. It's fun though when Holmes illustrates his great detective skills, such as a challenge by his smug school rival Dudley (Earl Rhodes).

"On this occasion, the entire school was bursting with excitement," narrates Hordern. "Dudley had challenged Holmes to a test of ingenuity, skill, and perception. Dudley had snatched the school's fencing trophy and hidden it in a secret place. He gave Holmes sixty minutes to find the trophy. Holmes accepted the challenge with confidence." As far as the rest of the cast goes, Nigel Stock is ok as Waxflatter, Holmes' eccentric mentor. "Retired schoolmaster," says Holmes of him. "Degrees in Chemistry and Biology, well versed in Philosophy, Mathematics and Physics. Author of 27 books." While Waxflatter's flying bike capers become slightly wearing after a while, the film has fun in inventing a source of inspiration to the young detective. "Elementary, my dear Holmes," says Waxflatter. "Elementary."

Sophie Ward is decent enough in a standard English Rose type of role and Anthony Higgins is quite suave as Holmes' urbane teacher and fencing master Rathe. As Watson, Alan Cox is likeable although the film does veer towards making him out to be something of a nerdy buffoon who is more likely to grow up to be Nigel Bruce than anyone else. The Victorian, slightly gothic school atmosphere with period uniforms, Watson's spectacles and general swirling air of mystery and adventure does actually make you wonder at times if Young Sherlock Holmes was an influence in some way on the Harry Potter universe and phenomenon.

I should mention Roger Ashton-Griffiths, who is quite a nice addition as a snotty Lestrade with little time for the speculations of the young Holmes. "Oh, not again," groans Lestrade when Holmes enters his office. "It's been a long time. Three, four days since your last visit? Just like last month when you were convinced that the French ambassador had embezzled 300 thousand pounds from the Bank of England?" It's a mildly amusing idea to speculate that the schoolboy Holmes pestered Lestrade with his theories and investigations - their paths to cross many, many times in future decades on numerous cases.

Young Sherlock Holmes is entertaining and mostly pleasant with some nice doffs of the cap to Conan Doyle and fun speculations on the early days of Holmes. It perhaps though tries a little too hard at times to be an effects driven popcorn summer blockbuster - an attitude that sometimes sits uncomfortably with the Victorian atmosphere and decent performances. This is a film that could have been so much better but it certainly has its moments and Rowe makes a fine youthful incarnation of Sherlock Holmes.

YULE NEVER LEAVE! - THE LEAGUE OF GENTLEMEN CHRISTMAS SPECIAL (2000)

Yule Never Leave! is The League of Gentlemen Christmas Special from 2000. This is arguably the best thing they ever did and the line between comedy and horror is blurred and beautifully juggled. The League of Gentlemen Christmas Special is both funny and scary in the end. Yule Never Leave! is an hour long and was directed by by Steve Bendelack.

The enjoyable thing about this special is the way that it serves as a loving homage to Amicus anthology horror films. Yule Never Leave! also taps into the way that Christmas can be a surprisingly great backdrop for horror. Who will ever forget Joan Collins being menaced in her house on Christmas Eve by an escaped maniac dressed as Father Christmas in 1972's Tales from the Crypt? Yule Never Leave! is cut from a similar cloth. Christmas is a scary time in this special episode of The League of Gentlemen.

Yule Never Leave! contains three horror tales - all framed by the foul mouthed and politically incorrect Reverend Bernice (Shearsmith) in her church. She is rather lacking in the Christmas spirit herself but will some unexpected visitors make her change her ways? The League of Gentlemen Christmas Special begins with Christmas music and snow but something is most definitely 'off' concerning this seasonal scene. This is a dark foreboding Christmas atmosphere. Something bad is going to happen.

This special was around the point where The League of Gentlemen dropped the 'laughter track' and moved away from its early sketch show feel. Yule Never Leave! not only feels ambitious but is a great piece of television in its own right. It is scary, well made, witty, and brilliantly acted by the cast. This special (and The League of Gentlemen generally) are an example of how Shearsmith and Pemberton can mesh the highbrow and lowbrow and the mundane and the fantastical all together in a way that other writers would struggle to achieve. It is something they would later do on Inside No. 9.

The first story has Charlie Hull (Pemberton) telling the tale of his exploits in a line-dancing competition and the intervention of a strange group known as 'Solutions' on behalf on his wife Stella (Shearsmith). Stella is desperate to stop him line-dancing - a premise so ridiculous it could only have come from this show! This segment is both amusing and creepy. It's funny when Stella attends a masked meeting of this secret society and can only find a Postman Pat mask to wear. Shearsmith and Pemberton are very funny as the bickering couple in the early scenes with double entendres ahoy.

The second story is a wonderfully dark and amusing segment where a man named Matthew recalls the time he was a young exchange student staying with German teacher Herr Lipp (Pemberton). Matthew had to fend off Lipp's desperate romantic advances but also deal with the suspicion that there was something not quite right about Lipp and perhaps the choir. This is a clever riff on vampire lore, German expressionism and old Hammer films. It is rife with sexual innuendo and risque lines but also quite scary when the twists arrive. This is a handsome looking segment too worthy of a feature film. There are some great nightmare sequences too that evoke An Amercian Werewolf in London.

Finally, we go back in time to learn why vet Mr Chinnery (Gatiss) seems to be forever accident prone when it comes to saving animals. This all stems from a family curse that dates back to the Victorian era. This Victorian ghost story riffs on The Monkey's Paw and is an affectionate (if darkly comic) homage to Hammer films and Frankenstein. The end wraparound goes back to Bernice and her nightmarish memories of how a bizarre figure (the scariest in the series for those who know who I'm talking about) kidnapped her mother dressed as Father Christmas.

Yule Never Leave! is very enjoyable for horror fans with the Gothic riffs on old Hammer and Amicus films and the clever screenplay. It might well be the finest hour of the The League of Gentlemen. If you are ever stuck for something spooky to watch at Halloween or Christmas and have never watched this before then you could a lot worse than try Yule Never Leave! This special episode remains a lot of fun with great production values and a memorable mixture of comedy and horror.

www.ingramcontent.com/pod-product-compliance
Lightning Source LLC
Chambersburg PA
CBHW021203130726
47988CB00002B/490